AMERICAN FOOD

AMERICAN FOOD

A *NOT-SO-SERIOUS* HISTORY

RACHEL WHARTON

with
illustrations by
KIMBERLY ELLEN HALL

ABRAMS IMAGE, NEW YORK

CONTENTS

INTRODUCTION
6

INTRODUCTION

It might seem like a silly time to look backward, just when American food is finally getting good. After a couple of dark decades of foods that were fast and frozen or French continental, this country's cooking isn't an international joke anymore, the kids' meal in the fancy restaurant of the world.

Oh, yeah, there are still plenty of arches and kings and huts on our highways. But there are also a whole lot of Americans psyched to taste regional traditions or indigenous flora and fauna, or to learn about cooking in neighborhoods and communities that were formerly ignored by everyone who didn't live in them. Maybe the biggest and best change is that a lot of us are now finally opening up to sharing a meal (or at least some flavors) with Other People Who Don't Look Like We Do.

As my friend Gabrielle made clear in her 2017 book on contemporary cooking in the United States—it's called *America: The Cookbook*, and it contains eight hundred recipes—American food today is not just "national standards," as in hot dogs and meat loaf and mashed potatoes. Which is why in her book you'll also find recipes for American foods like falafel, plantain chips, pho, and injera.

But this book does not document our ever-evolving future, even though that is a very delicious thing to do. This one reconsiders our past. And with a focus on things so common that they might not even seem so interesting, at least at first. You may think you already know all there is to learn about Buffalo wings, eggs Benedict, submarines and hoagies and heros, yellow mustard, Green Goddess salad dressing, or even shrimp and grits. You might think they have little to say about who we are becoming, foodwise, or even who we are today.

BUT OLD THINGS NEARLY ALWAYS tell new stories. In fact, I should admit that my collaborator Kim and I chose our subjects at random, more or less—picking one well-known American food item for every letter in the alphabet. We had guessed that almost any food eaten in this country would have a multilayered history, some forgotten twists and turns. Thankfully, we were right.

NOW, LET'S SEE WHAT WE EAT

And Kim was the perfect partner, as her art helps tell new stories, too. Her own work has always focused on the beauty of the ordinary—the seemingly mundane little items of the kitchen, the old community cookbooks set out with the recycling. We believe the history of American food is a lot like those community cookbooks, full of half-remembered stories and substitutions that have spiraled off into their own thing. Like those books, Kim's hand-drawn illustrations have a rough, human vibe that brings a human connection to stories about a very human topic: food.

Maybe I should warn you that not all these new stories are 100 percent positive—which is maybe why they're the stories we should be telling the most. A lot of times in the not-so-distant past, we didn't give credit where credit was due. We forced and we stole. We ignored. We dismissed, we straight-up dissed. We even corralled and encamped. And we tend to assume what we think we know about all the latter is true.

"WE" IS OFTEN ME. As in, a white American with Colonial-era roots in this country. I don't really have another home country or culture to identify with, unlike a growing majority of Americans. I resemble the sentiments expressed by social historian Alfred Crosby in the introduction to his thirtieth-anniversary reissue of *The Columbian Exchange*. He wrote that over the years he learned that "people who didn't look like me had been appallingly mistreated by people who did look like me . . . and there were big pieces missing from the kind of history I was teaching." He also makes the point that looking at commonly accepted things from a new perspective is "like replacing the standard film in your camera with infrared or ultraviolet film. You see things you have never seen before."

And so it was for us, working on this book. I hope it'll be the same for you.

A

AMBROSIA

I know what you're thinking. How deep can a book go that begins with a fluffy fruit salad called ambrosia, whose most controversial element is whether you go mayonnaise or whipped topping instead of mini marshmallows? And, actually, that is kind of a big deal for traditionalists who consider the ur-ambrosia to be orange slices, white sugar, and hand-grated fresh coconut, as per the nineteenth-century original.

Those ingredients were still expensive when Maria Massey Barringer published the first known recipe in her 1867 cookbook, *Dixie Cookery*. Coconut and oranges were rare, and even the sugar may have had to be prepped and pounded because it came in a giant loaf rather than cubed or granulated.

But Maria, who perhaps optimistically subtitled her work a *Practical Cook-Book for Southern Housekeepers*, could probably afford it. She and her husband—a lawyer, state senator, and major in the Confederate army—would have been boldfaced names in Maria's Old South town of Concord, North Carolina. In fact, she once hosted a dinner with Jefferson Davis, the president of the Confederate States of America, when he crashed at her home with nearly a dozen members of his posse while fleeing Virginia after General Robert E. Lee surrendered to the Union Army in 1865. Though Maria's cook, Ellen—almost certainly an enslaved woman whose freedom Davis was fighting to deny—was the one who had to make it.

WE KNOW THIS from a letter Maria wrote to her sister years later:

> *I had a few minutes talk with Ellen (the cook) who told me she had just taken from the oven a large loaf of rolls and one of our largest hams and these supplemented by poultry and vegetables and a*

tipsy cake pudding and fruits with cream furnished the simple dinner, ready in a half hour after their arrival.

And this is where things start to get contentious: Like most wealthy white women in the Old South at the time, said Helen Zoe Veit, an expert on antebellum American food and a professor of history at Michigan State University, Maria might have known what to ask for on the table, but most likely couldn't cook it. The well-off, even those without plantations, owned at least a few slaves until emancipation. They also employed black domestic servants afterward, when they "pretty quickly ended up back on top of the social ladder," said Veit, who included an explicated version of *Dixie Cookery* (and some of Maria's letter) in her series of books on food in the Civil War.

"Almost certainly" most of Maria's recipes were told to her by Ellen, Veit explained to me, adding that Maria wrote much of the book during the early 1860s, during the Civil War. As an enslaved woman, Ellen couldn't write them down herself—by law, she couldn't be taught to read and write. So Maria's book, said Veit, could be considered born not of pride or practicality, but also self-preservation. As in, lose your slaves, you lose your recipes, too.

Ellen doesn't even rate a mention in Maria's book. (This is true of nearly every cookbook until 1904, according to food writer and scholar Toni Tipton-Martin, who has written extensively about black and African cooks and American food history.) In fact, Maria's introduction made the false and "racist assertion common at the time," said Veit, that as a white Southern homemaker, her duties were even more complicated than those of her Northern contemporaries, even though she grew up with a lot of built-in labor. Maria wrote that:

There is a very mistaken notion at the North and West, about the domestic life of Southerners, Southern women especially. The common idea is, that we are entirely destitute of practical knowledge of household affairs. This is a great mistake. The contrary is true. A Southern woman must know how to prepare any dish, for she finds no cooks made to order; they must be of her own training, in the minutest particulars of every department.

AMBROSIA

"GRATE THE WHITE
PART OF THE
COCOANUT, SWEETEN
WITH A LITTLE
SUGAR, AND PLACE
IN A GLASS BOWL, IN
ALTERNATE LAYERS
WITH PULPED ORANGES,
HAVING A LAYER
OF COCOANUT ON TOP.
SERVE IN ICE-CREAM
PLATES OR SAUCERS."
 - DIXIE COOKERY
1867

TO CRACK A COCONUT
START WITH A MATURE
BROWN COCONUT-HOLD IT
IN ONE HAND, THEN USE
THE DULL BACK SIDE OF
A CLEAVER TO GIVE THE
COCONUT A FEW HARD
TAPS ALONG ITS THREE
LONGITUDINAL GROOVES
JUST UNTIL THE SHELL
CRACKS OPEN. WORK OVER
A BOWL TO CATCH THE
COCONUT WATER. BREAK
THE COCONUT APART INTO
PIECES, THEN USE A PARING
KNIFE TO CUT THE MEAT
AWAY FROM THE SHELL
IN CHUNKS.

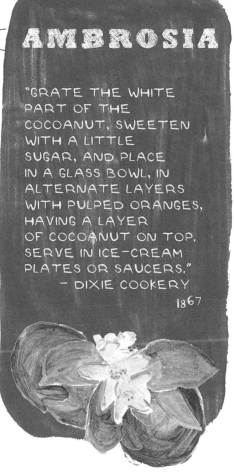

Ancient-food historian Andrew Coletti helped me crack the code to this recipe.
He reminded me that the original ambrosia was a liquid-solid compound eaten by
the Greek gods. Today we might read the above and just peel an orange and
layer the resulting segments with sugar and coconut, but Maria Massey Barringer's
instructions are probably telling us to remove all peel and pith and even slightly
macerate the individual pieces of pulp. The result is both delicious and liquid-solid:
just like the mythical one. For maximum impact you should also use freshly grated
coconut, powdered sugar as many recipes did in the early 1900s, and preferably
oranges in season, aka winter.

ST. AUGUSTINE

The first oranges in the country came before it was one: In the sixteenth century, Spanish conquistadors planted trees in what would become St. Augustine on the northeastern coast of Florida.

OF COURSE WE DON'T KNOW FOR SURE if Ellen had a hand in ambrosia's ideation. Maria did thank "an English friend" for many of her recipes, but given the rampant copying and lack of effusive headnotes in cookbooks in this period of history, not to mention the lack of Southern books from this period at all, said Veit, we may never know who really invented it, unless we come across some previously unknown letter or text.

We do know that there were similar sliced-orange salads in cookbooks before this one. It could have been Maria's idea to add the coconut, it could have been the English friend's idea, and it could also have been Ellen's idea. (This is intriguing when you consider that the enslaved were of West or Central African and possibly West Indian descent and likely knew a hell of a lot more about "cocoa-nuts" than Maria did.) Like most other cookbook authors of the time, Maria didn't even think to tell her readers how to open a fresh one, probably because she'd never had to do it herself.

Given Maria's light experience in the kitchen, she might even have appreciated modern-day ambrosias made entirely of industrialized, processed foods—things that are already canned, cut or bagged, served for very little money and with even less labor. If the first additions to ambrosia were modest, a little sherry and pineapple and banana or pecans and coconut milk, by the mid-twentieth century, recipe books show no restraint. (See the 2016 NPR story: "When Ambrosia Salad Spells Dread.")

By the mid-twentieth century, noted Veit, ambrosia had gone from "this impossibly hard-to-source recipe for people" to something "so democratized." Today it's made across the country, eaten by all colors and classes, and served from the buffet table at grand Southern mansions and from the salad bar at all-you-can-eat buffets.

Which should serve as a gentle reminder to all the haters of canned fruit and Cool Whip that the modern form of ambrosia doesn't represent status, but freedom.

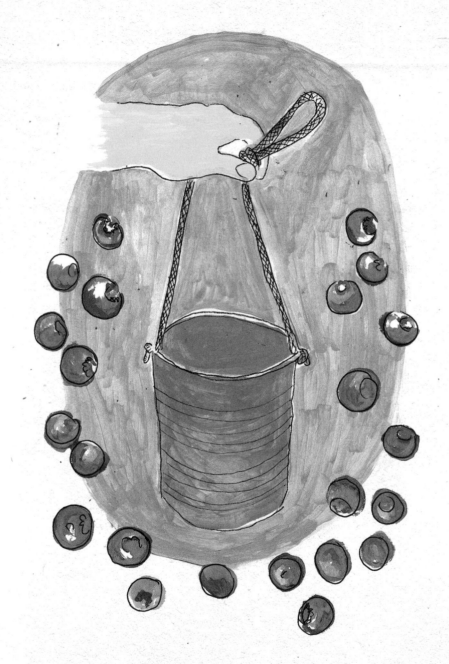

THE WHITE BLUSH

B

BLUEBERRIES

If you take the time to drive the smaller byways of the South New Jersey Pinelands—a multi-county area that includes a million preserved acres of sugar sand, pitch pine, and white cedar—you'll find Stevens Blueberries, a seven-acre commercial operation at the end of a white sand road deep in the pine forests of New Lisbon.

When Richard and Connie Stevens bought their small farm in the 1980s, it came with a blueberry hoeing machine made from Ford Model A parts. It also came with some equally old bushes. The farm is now run by their son, Richard Stevens Jr., and the family sells their crop to a packer but also allows pick-your-own. Visitors can still see what was planted there in 1951, said the younger Mr. Stevens, including seventy-year-old Elizabeths, Stanleys, Weymouths, Berkeleys, Bluecrops, and Jerseys, plus a few Rancocas that are off limits.

"THEY'RE MY MOM'S PRIDE AND JOY," said Stevens. "We're not allowed to touch them."

They were once the pride and joy of Elizabeth Coleman White, the cranberry farmer's daughter who literally founded the industry in 1916. Until then, blueberries were still a wild thing, an indigenous American fruit foraged like ramps or morels. White made taming the northern highbush berries growing in her woods her life's work, making American agricultural history in the process. Like cranberries, blueberries thrive in acidic soil, which the Pinelands have in spades.

"They were really looking for a second crop for cranberry growers," said Allison Pierson, director of the Whitesbog Preservation Trust, a

---

Opposite: Many New Jersey pick-your-own operations still stock the old blue pails that you can tie around your waist. Berries straight from the bush will still have their pale-white coating—a white blush that slips away as the fruit travels from place to place.

ELIZABETH COLEMAN WHITE

CRANBERRIES, ANOTHER AMERICAN FRUIT, WERE THE GATEWAY CROP FOR BLUEBERRY GROWERS

E. C. White was the founder of the cultivated blueberry, though she didn't do it all on her own. She owes a debt of gratitude both to Frederick Vernon Coville, the US government botanist who partnered with her on her cultivation work, and to the many blacks, Puerto Ricans, and Italian Americans who came from South Philadelphia each summer to pick berries on her father's huge property, living on the land plantation-style.

nonprofit that runs the three-thousand-acre White family farm now preserved inside New Jersey's Brendan T. Byrne State Forest. Known as Whitesbog Historic Village, it includes the Whites' original berries, like the long-forgotten Katherines, Junes, Pembertons, Dixis, and Warehams still planted around her house. (Yes, said Pierson, you can pick them.)

White, who died in 1954, also helped launch Tru-Blu Cooperative Association to distribute and market the fruit across the country, said Pierson, complete with New York City subway ads and fruit-forward galas at B. Altman and Company's Fifth Avenue department store.

Their first order of business was just to get people to call them blueberries. Mark Ehlenfeldt, a blueberry breeding specialist with the United States Department of Agriculture in nearby Chatsworth who moonlights as the newsletter editor for Whitesbog, said that originally, most people called any blue berry a huckleberry, technically a different plant.

BOTANICALLY SPEAKING, there are three types of blueberries, said Ehlenfeldt: highbush, lowbush—still only wild and most famous in Maine—and rabbiteye. Those have fewer "sparkling notes" and are traditionally found in the south, though Ehlenfeldt has quite a few in his vast research collection.

In truth, nearly all nonwild blueberries now in New Jersey, if not most farmed around the world, can be directly traced back to White's work. Many of the more interesting farms around here can, too.

A few miles west of Whitesbog, for example, is Haines Berry Farm, run by the great-grandson of the Whitesbog superintendent. And just across the road, you'll find Pine Barrens Native Fruits, run by White's great-nephew Joe Darlington.

The Darlingtons lease and farm the cranberry bogs at Whitesbog and care for several acres of Elizabeths. Released in 1966 and named after White—who considered it to have exquisite flavor—the Elizabeth is a cult favorite, said Pine Barrens Native Fruits staffer Connie Casselman. She alerts their mailing list when the fruits, which can grow to the size of a quarter, are for sale.

"They're the sweetest berry you'll ever have," said Casselman. "People come from all over to get them."

DUKES, BLUECROPS, AND ELLIOTTS are now the three big berries in New Jersey, said Mr. Ehlenfeldt. All three are high-yield varieties that can also withstand disease and shipping, which is why they're what Joe Badiacco, the owner of Rosedale Blueberry Farm, grows on his thirty organic acres in Hammonton, the heart of the Pinelands blueberry industry. Like those of most New Jersey growers, Badiacco's berries all ripen in just a five-week period: the Dukes in June, the Bluecrops by July, and then the smaller, tarter Elliotts finish out the season.

DREAMY CREAMS

MELTING VANILLA
ICE CREAM

ICE CREAM
CONE

BLUEBERRIES

for fresh blues

1. SOUR CREAM SPICED WITH NUTMEG & A TOUCH OF ORANGE MARMALADE
2. SWEETENED WHIPPED CREAM WITH CRUSHED PINEAPPLE OR SLIVERS OF FRESH MINT
3. SOFT ICE CREAM MIXED WITH FINELY CHOPPED CRYSTALLIZED GINGER

ADAPTED FROM "24 LUSCIOUS BLUEBERRY RECIPES" BY THE TRU-BLU COOPERATIVE ASSOCIATION, CIRCA 1927

Badiacco's operation may be bigger than the Stevenses', but he's still small compared to the average grower in the state, which has at least a hundred acres. "It seems like the days of mom-and-pops like myself are ending," said Badiacco: Today, he said, farmers and packers are buying up smaller farms like his, accumulating acres across the region, and moving to machine picking.

At the same time, New Jersey went from the country's number-one blueberry producer to one eclipsed by states like Washington, Oregon, Michigan, California, and Georgia. "But that's as far as acreage goes," said Badiacco, reminding me that the Pinelands acidic soils keep his berries at the top of a much more impressive list. "Now, as far as taste is concerned," he said, "that's New Jersey."

*Parts of this story originally appeared in the *New York Times*.

C
CLAMS

If you're not from Massachusetts, it might seem nuts to pay nearly twenty-five dollars for a platter of fried whole belly clams and French fries from the clapboard Cape Cod institution called Kream 'n' Kone, where you order from a counter and eat off paper plates.

But those who are from Massachusetts—or Maine, New Hampshire, Rhode Island, eastern Connecticut, or even the tip of New York's Long Island, all places where clam shacks like the Kream 'n' Kone are common—understand that fried belly clams are a summer necessity, even when they're twice the price of lobster.

Whole belly clams are not the same clams you get stuffed or served on the half shell. (Those are hardshell clams like littlenecks, aka *Mercenaria mercenaria*.) They are not fried clam strips, which aren't whole clams but translucent slices of the chewy foot or tongue of the giant Atlantic surf clam, or *Spisula solidissima*. (Their big bellies get ground up for chowder.)

BELLY CLAMS MEANS SOFTSHELL CLAMS, aka piss clams, aka Ipswich clams, aka the thin-and-brittle-shelled wide-mouthed clam with a long, wriggly siphon technically known as *Mya arenaria*. Softshell clams must be dug by hand at low tide, raked from the muddy flats of tidal rivers, bays, and sounds—they're found further south on the East Coast, but taste best up where it's coldest—then shucked, battered, and fried, belly, siphon, and all.

"They're a delicacy," said Angela Argyriadis, who runs the Kream 'n' Kone in West Dennis, Massachusetts, with her husband, Angelo.

At left, a tray of fried belly clams and a bowl of lobster bisque at the Kreme 'n' Kone, which opened in 1953. Like many who work in the Massachusetts clamming industry, its owners are of Greek descent.

They're twenty-five dollars not just because they're hand-raked and sort of fragile—their gaping shells are hard to ship whole, and the bellies tend to burst when you freeze them, said Argyriadis—but also because they're slowly disappearing.

"EVERYWHERE YOU GO, LANDINGS ARE DOWN," said Clyde L. MacKenzie, a shellfish researcher with the US National Marine Fisheries Service lab in New Jersey. *Landings* is the term for how many clams are harvested commercially, and MacKenzie is uniquely qualified to study them. He has spent the better part of five decades studying bivalves and grew up in Martha's Vineyard, where he sold softshells for ten dollars a bushel in 1950.

Between that same year and 1980, according to a 2018 paper MacKenzie coauthored, clammers experienced the traditional ups and downs of the industry. But things started to change in 1980. That's when the numbers of softshells—along with other bivalves like wild oysters, scallops, and hardshell clams—started to decline in every single state where they're collected.

Clammers, restaurateurs, and other industry types have offered up plenty of reasons for the loss of softshells in recent decades. Those include (*a*) we're taking too many and they don't bounce back, (*b*) pollution is closing too many areas to harvest, and (*c*) there are fewer professional fisherfolk to rake them as working waterfronts transform into hotels, high-end marinas, and restaurants. But MacKenzie's paper showed *a* was wrong, and *b* and *c* were only partial explanations.

There is instead a much more pervasive problem. You could lump it all under "habitat degradation," said MacKenzie, but it's really a slew of interrelated climate and environmental issues that tend to build off one another. These include warmer, less saline waters that make it hard for clams to thrive; algal blooms that are poisonous to people; rainwater runoff from storms that carries pollution or lowers salinity; plus an increase in clam-eating predators like green crabs, fish, and worms that thrive in these conditions. These are compounded during periods when the North Atlantic Oscillation Index is positive (as in much of the past three decades) and the ocean gets even warmer on its own.

To top it all off, MacKenzie's study noted, fewer clams eventually does lead to fewer clammers, which means even fewer whole bellies make it to the market.

A HUNDRED FIFTY YEARS AGO, the story was just the opposite. In 1887, even the *Washington Progress* paper in North Carolina was remarking on the abundance of clams in the Ipswich and Essex flats of Massachusetts, which was already the most famous clam terroir in the state. "They lie so thickly packed together in the mud and are so easily gathered," a correspondent reported, "that even a green hand at clam digging can easily earn $4 per day at the work."

CLAMMING

CLAMS

CLAMMING
TOOLS

SHELLING
CLAMS

Though you'll often read about how Ipswich and Essex produce the best-tasting clams for one reason or another—the mud, maybe, or the richness of the local algae the clams eat—these two towns likely became the heart of the clamming industry for more practical reasons, said MacKenzie: "They had a lot of clams." The towns share especially "big muddy broad flats," he said, "you could walk out a quarter mile."

(Currently MacKenzie favors clams from Maine, because the high salinity of the cold waters makes for healthy, good-tasting shellfish. Which is why even though the softshell habitat runs all the way south to North Carolina, nobody eats them south of New York.)

ORIGINALLY, IPSWICH AND ESSEX clams went by train to Boston and other cities. But with the invention of the car and the fried clam shack, the city started to come to the clams.

This may or may not have gotten its start in 1916, when Bessie Woodman started frying the clams her husband, Lawrence, dug in Essex. Though they incorrectly say they were the first to ever fry a clam—which any cursory review of early American newspapers and cookbooks easily disproves—Woodman's of Essex definitely did something right. (Maybe it was to create the "Ipswich style" of clam, which is dipped in evaporated milk, battered in a mixture of corn and white flour, and fried in lard.)

By 1959, there were dozens of fried clam shacks on the road around Ipswich Bay. Edgar J. Driscoll Jr. in his travel column called "Wish You Were Here," raved about Woodman's in particular, which employed fifty people at three establishments that served 2,500 people on Sunday during the peak season. (His article, by the way, simply says the Woodmans were the first to fry clams in Essex.)

EVEN THEN, IT WAS AN OPEN SECRET that demand for Massachusetts softshells was already outstripping supply. "A lot of people here don't like to admit it, but 75 percent of the fried clams come out of Maryland," Lawrence Woodman's grandson Dexter told the *Boston Globe* in 1972. After Maryland's softshells were destroyed by a tropical storm that year that changed the salinity in the Chesapeake, they came out of Maine.

In the 1950s the Soffron Brothers Clam Company in Ipswich—then the sole supplier for Massachusetts-based Howard Johnson's, whose growing chain of restaurants advertised fried clams on their roadside signs—invented the "Tendersweet" surf clam strip during a softshell shortage.

By 1994, Peter Maistrellis of Ipswich Maritime Products considered that Ipswich clams had become like French fried potatoes. "Do they come from France?" Maistrellis asked. "No, they're a style of food. Ipswich clams are a certain species cooked in a certain fashion." (Ipswich Maritime, by the way, is still one of the largest seafood distribution companies in Ipswich. It's where restaurants like Kream 'n' Kone get theirs.)

If in those days restaurants tipped off customers when their clams weren't from the mud flats nearby, today it's the reverse. You'll see Ipswich clams on menus all over the East Coast, but if you want them dug locally when you're in Massachusetts, "native clams" is what to look for . . . Though natives might be even more expensive than "imported" ones.

Unless we see a good run of very cold winters, said MacKenzie, which will help tamp down disease and all those other issues, don't expect softshells to get any cheaper. There will likely always be plenty of them for the semiprofessional digger and the Northeasterner with a clam rake in their back pocket, but some seafood restaurant owners already predict that whole belly clams will soon be sold just like raw oysters. As in, a bargain when you find them for a buck apiece.

EAST COAST CLAMS

 CHERRYSTONE

TOPNECK

 MIDDLENECK

 LITTLENECK

MAHOGANY

 SOFTSHELL aka steamer

ATLANTIC JACKKNIFE CLAM aka razor clam

WEST COAST AND ALASKAN CLAMS

PACIFIC LITTLENECK aka rock cockle

BUTTER

RAZOR

Littleneck clams—technically the Atlantic littleneck—are the same kind of clam as the topneck, cherrystone, and quahog. All are just varying sizes of Atlantic hardshell clams. Softshells are also found in the mud in the Pacific Northwest, but there and in Alaska the similar-ish Pacific razor is the more coveted local clam.

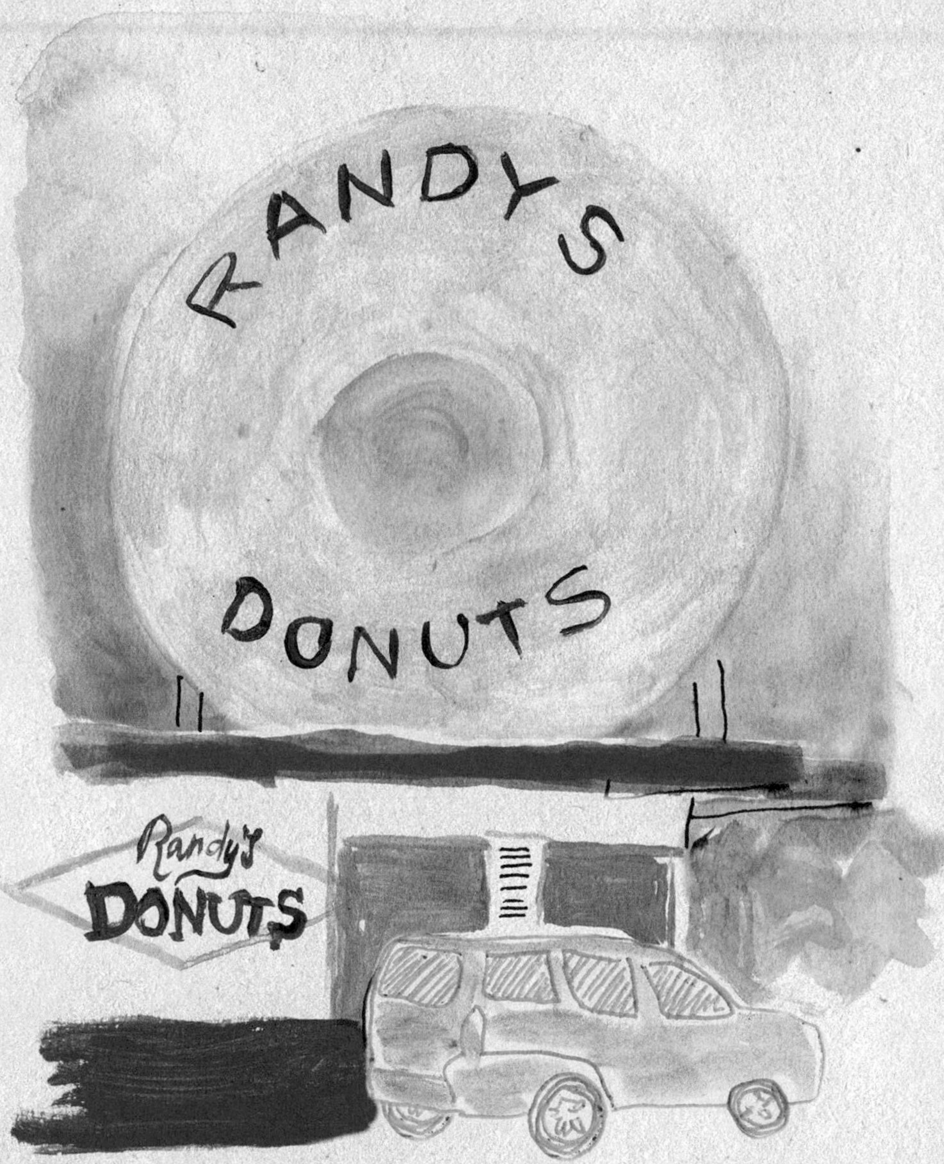
RANDYS
DONUTS
Randy's
DONUTS

DONUTS

Alexis Iammarino did not set out to be one of the greatest living experts on American donut history. And she would argue that she isn't, that she's just a curator, a connector. Yet somehow this visual artist, who co-owns a gallery in Rockland, Maine, became, at the age of thirty-six, the keeper of American donut history.

This began by accident in 2013. The short story is this: While working on a public mural of Rockland city history, Iammarino meets with the Rockland Historical Society, finds out that while the American donut is most likely a descendant of the Dutch *olykoek*, Rockland lays claim to the hole. It was said to be invented in 1847 by Hanson Crockett Gregory, a Maine schooner captain who lived in what was then called Clam Cove, just outside of town. ("I was flabbergasted," Iammarino wrote of the moment, "that such a claim could be singularly attributed to one place or individual.")

At which point Iammarino—who once worked as a pastry chef and admits to a love for desserts—embarked on a plan to have an art exhibit based on the donut hole, sent out a call for work about donuts, and ended up with 250 submissions. "I documented everything that came my way," she told me. "I kept getting so many submissions. . . . It was like, so now what do I have on my hands?"

THE ANSWER WAS a near-complete history of the donut in America, in artistic, literary, and academic forms. This was all displayed at her art gallery and in other places in Rockland, but, more importantly, captured in *Hole History: Origins of the American-Style Donut*, the post-show catalog Iammarino created with her gallery cofounder, Maeve O'Regan.

When Iammarino started out, her goal was not so much to learn the history of the hole but to bring together people who had made it the focus of their work, and maybe to highlight the funny ironies

ROCKLAND
MAINE

in the mythical origin stories a lot of small-town tourism is built on. Still, if you listen to Iammarino talk donut tidbits—like the year the first mass-produced donut cutter was invented ten miles south in nearby Thomaston (1872); the minute details of eighteenth-century recipes; the need for cheap and filling food for industrial workers and its effect on donut technology and culture; or the philosophical role of donuts in any discussion of American dietary issues—you'll quickly see that the artist now knows quite a bit about the old donut herself.

BUT DONUTS ARE LIKE THAT. They'll draw you in. As historian Sandy Oliver put it in her introduction to Iammarino's book: "We do not mythologize, tell jokes, or debate about unimportant dishes. The more significant a dish or food item is, the more common are wide variations of recipes for it, claims about its origins, and frequency of it on menus, or ubiquity of sales. According to these characteristics, doughnuts definitely qualify as significant."

Just look at what happened to Fred E. Crockett, said Iammarino, who devoted an entire appendix in her book to his important body of donut research.

A distant relative of Hanson Crockett Gregory, Fred Crockett was a former Boy Scout administrator and skilled raconteur who, upon

CRAZIEST DONUTS

| blueberry bourbon basil | cointreau crème brûlée | birthday cake |

neon tiger | cranberry gingersnap | fig labneh

FIRST TWO FROM BLUE STAR DONUTS IN PORTLAND OREGON. SECOND TWO FROM THE DONUT PUB IN NYC. LAST TWO FROM FEDERAL DONUTS IN PHILADELPHIA. ACTUAL DONUT APPEARANCE WILL VARY!

learning more about his elder's contribution to cuisine, made promoting it his life's work. He tracked down competing stories, sent out angry letters, took part in parades, and was asked to attend the 1940 World's Fair, whose theme was the future—and this apparently included donut holes. There he unveiled a statue of Captain Gregory. The following year, he debated a Cape Cod attorney who claimed that the real hole came from an Indian who had shot an arrow through a pilgrim's fried dough.

"This guy spent his entire life as the donut ambassador to Maine, one of his self-proclaimed titles," said Iammarino. In fact, her pink and green book is an homage to the little book on the subject that he published himself.

THE SMITHSONIAN NATIONAL MUSEUM OF AMERICAN HISTORY HAS A LARGE STORE OF DONUT ARTIFACTS,
INCLUDING (AT LEFT) MATERIALS FROM THE SALLY L. STEINBERG COLLECTION OF DOUGHNUT EPHEMERA
AND (AT RIGHT) A 1950S AUTOMATIC DONUT MACHINE MADE FROM KRISPY KREME.

NOW THEN, ABOUT THAT HOLE.

Real food history experts like to pick apart the Gregory story,
which the captain told to the *Boston Evening Record* in 1916. They sniff
about how holes in foods are commonly in all of our consciousness,
and how other recipes of the time suggest making fry cakes in a ring, and
how ascribing this or any other food invention to one single person
is silly—you can read many of their well-researched opinions in extreme
detail in *The Hole History*.

That is likely true—fried dough is ancient and ubiquitous, and so
are holes.

But if the captain didn't invent the literal hole, his story certainly put
us on the path to where it is now. Consider his fame, and that his relative
made the hole a thing of American pride at the 1940 World's Fair and
festivals in the 1950s, and countless TV shows and newspapers onward,
up to Iammarino's revival. Not to mention Rockport's proximity to
Boston, now the corporate donut capital of the world, thanks to Dunkin'.

I do believe the donut as the world knows it now—many shapes and colors, stuffed with custard and topped with sprinkles and sold 24/7 and made with the hole—is all-American. And for that, we can certainly give Captain Gregory his due, along with the city of Rockland and now, of course, Alexis Iammarino.

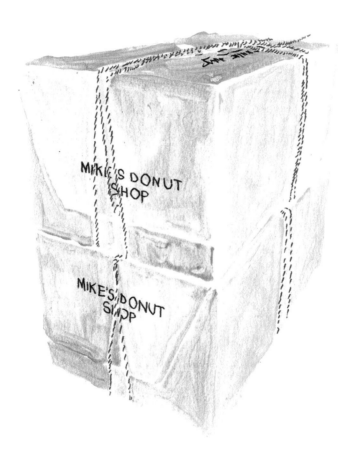

At Mike's Donuts in Brooklyn, every donut is still cut by hand. Greek immigrant Mike Neamonitis started the shop as a wholesale operation in a former ice cream parlor after learning the trade under another Greek donut maker. John T. Edge, in his book *Donuts: An American Passion*, drives home how small, seemingly ordinary neighborhood donut shops help fulfill the American dream. Start-up costs are low, it's a cash business, and everyone loves donuts.

how to build
EGGS BENEDICT

English Muffin

Canadian Bacon

Poached Egg Hollandaise Sauce

EGGS BENEDICT

If getting to the bottom of a Benedict weren't already difficult enough—there are invention stories from several Benedicts, most of them scant and secondhand, plus some confusing cookbooks—then you find out about "The Rich Fool and the Clever Pauper."

That's the name of an 1894 work of fiction by Horace Annesley Vachell, a British expatriate then living in San Francisco. Printed in the January issue of *Overland Monthly*, a California literary magazine, it is considered to be the first-known printed reference to eggs à la Benedict, as poached eggs over toast with ham and hollandaise was originally known.

And I quote: "After luncheon, which consisted of Blue Points, potted char, *eggs à la Benedict*, and a remarkable Maraschino jelly, Jimmy announced his intention of taking a walk by himself."

Jimmy was the fictional rich fool, and he was dining at the University Club in San Francisco, which was a real fancy club. Blue Point oysters and potted char and fancy jellies were delicacies known to rich white people on both coasts back then, and thus we can assume that *eggs à la Benedict* were already known, too.

Now, remember that date of publication—January 1894—while you consider the three slim pieces of data that form the foundation of every account of the legend of eggs Benedict published in recent history. (Though most writers tend to embellish the retelling with their own creative details.)

EGGS BENEDICT EVIDENCE, PART ONE: There is the Lemuel Benedict at the Waldorf story, which appeared in *The New Yorker* in 1942, two years before Lemuel's death. By his own account to the reporter, the New York City socialite and stockbroker invented the dish forty-eight years earlier by ordering a similar concoction while hungover at the hotel. That could have been 1893, given that these were recollections, but no earlier, as the hotel only opened that year. Note: Lemuel preferred bacon and toast, rather than ham and an English muffin, but the latter was, he told *The New Yorker*, added to the hotel's repertoire by Oscar, the hotel's famous maître d', who used to work at Delmonico's, as mentioned below in "Eggs Benedict Evidence, Part Three."

EGGS BENEDICT EVIDENCE, PART TWO: The Commodore E. C. Benedict recipe story, from a column by *New York Times* food editor Craig Claiborne in 1967. A writer from Paris sent Claiborne a version of the recipe (ham plus toast plus hollandaise with a hard-boiled egg), along with the story that he got it from his mother, who got it from her brother, who was a friend of its inventor, the Commodore. E.C. was a New York City stockbroker who would have been hanging out among the other socialites in the 1890s. (Side note: By all accounts E.C. was kind of amazing, even if he didn't invent eggs Benedict.)

EGGS BENEDICT EVIDENCE, PART THREE: The Mrs. Le Grand Benedict at Delmonico's story. This is from a letter to the *New York Times* by Mabel C. Butler in response to the above. According to her family's lore, Mrs. Benedict was a relative of the commodore, and she created the dish at the "turn of the century" (Mabel's words) at then-world-famous Delmonico's, Mrs. Benedict's regular Saturday brunch spot. Mrs. Benedict told the maître'd what she wanted, in Mabel's telling, essentially the dish as we know it topped with some truffles. This letter is likely the sole thing backing up a 1978 *Bon Appétit* article called "Perfect Eggs Benedict," which enshrined the Le Grand Benedict story in American food history. This article so bothered Lemuel's first cousin once removed that he began fighting for his relative's alleged role in food history during the 1980s. He eventually amassed a de facto eggs Benny museum at his house in Colorado and earned, after his death, a 2007 story about his efforts in the *New York Times*, appropriately titled "Was He the Eggman?"

AND THAT LEADS TO A FEW QUESTIONS.
So for Horace Annesley Vachell to publish his piece in January 1894, eggs à la Benedict would have already had to have been the cutting

edge of fashion in late 1893. But why didn't the 1894 version of Charles Ranhofer's *The Epicurean*, the Delmonico's cookbook that features seemingly every recipe ever served at the restaurant and every menu in its 1,183 pages, add the recipe until its second printing in 1912? For that matter why didn't Oscar's 1896 Waldorf cookbook include it either? And neither place had it on early menus preserved from the era, to boot.

The first written recipe appears in 1897 in the February issue of *Table Talk* magazine. It was written by Cornelia C. Bedford, former principal of the New York Cooking School, in response to a reader request from Savannah, Georgia.

In truth, all these Benedicts would have eaten at Delmonico's and the Waldorf, and anyone who cooked for them anywhere else would have been privy to what they were eating at those places as well. By the time "Eggs à la Benedick" was added to *The Epicurean* (spelled with a *k*, just to make it even more confusing), the dish had already been celebrated in the catering, hotel management, and cooking magazines that spread trends among the cooks for the rich and those who aspired to cook like them.

Maybe it doesn't matter who the first Benedict really was. The real point, as has been said by many others in the past, is that this was a rich

dish devised for rich people, and all the creation myths just make it seem even more exclusive—some off-the-menu request made on the fly for a boldfaced name.

As Claiborne noted in his 1967 account, "Eggs Benedict is conceivably the most sophisticated dish ever created in America." It's also one that so retains its decadent luster that it remains a very modern dish today, destined for an eternity of brunches.

POSTSCRIPT: WHAT DO I THINK?

From what I can tell from census records, Mrs. Le Grand Benedict was actually Emma Frances Gardner Le Grand Benedict. She was a college graduate, writer, and newspaper journalist who in 1887 wrote a charming memoir from her time at the front of the Civil War when she was a newlywed.

I like to imagine that the creator of Eggs à la Benedict was a woman, at a time when Delmonico's was the first place to let them dine by themselves. (It was a women's press club that had their first ladies' supper there, another point in Mrs. Le Grand Benedict's favor.) Plus, maybe she knew old Horace Vachell, as they were both writers. Maybe she knew Cornelia Bedford. Either way, she was definitely bold enough to ask for exactly what she wanted for brunch.

The first printed recipe for eggs à la Benedict called for toast in 1897; the second, in hotel chef Adolphe Meyer's 1898 work *Eggs and How to Use Them*, called for a muffin. In ye olden times, the English muffin was just a muffin—Samuel Bath Thomas hadn't yet made the term *English muffin* a household name. Thomas, an Englishman in New York, opened his bakery on Ninth Avenue in Manhattan in 1880, and his expansion around the corner (shown opposite) is now a condo called the Muffin House. It's unclear when Canadian bacon became more popular than ham—though it likely came after food scientist and McDonald's executive Herbert Ralph Peterson invented the Egg McMuffin, the fast-food chain's version of eggs Benedict, in 1972. Ironically for a Gilded Age dish, the McMuffin was America's first fast-food breakfast sandwich.

F

FORTUNE COOKIE

If there's a mecca for fortune cookies, it's not in China (where they don't exist) but in San Francisco, at the northern end of the sidewalk-sized Ross Alley in Chinatown. It's where you'll find the Golden Gate Fortune Cookie Factory, founded in 1956 by Franklin Yee and his family.

Unlike most factories—if a cookie-crammed and memorabilia-cluttered storefront can be considered a factory—it is always open to tour groups and the curious public, who generally spill out the door. The crowd is thickest around the ladies who fill and fold still-warm wafers that emerge one after another from the ovens, a battery of rotating cast-iron contraptions that belch steam and are fed with a pitcher of liquid batter. Visitors can eat as many rejected cookies as they like for free—if you're only used to the takeout variety, these are toasty, nutty, crisp, barely sweet, still warm, and unexpectedly delicious—though you have to pay 50 cents to take a picture.

Golden Gate is not the first place in the country to make fortune cookies, and it may not even be the best. But it is the only place where you can see fortune cookies being made in America as they were nearly a century ago, a piece of living history. "I treat this business as a museum," said Yee's nephew Kevin Chan. "I want to show it to people.... This is culture, this is something that's from the past."

Though that past may be more complicated than it appears: Fortune cookies may are now easily mass-produced across the country—a fact made possible by the fully automated Fortune VII, patented by a Korean American in 1981—but the original idea came from the Japanese.

At Golden Gate Fortune Cookie Factory in San Francisco's Chinatown, still-warm wafers are delivered to staffers from the semiautomated ovens built in 1956.

YOU MAY HAVE ALREADY BEEN AWARE that the fortune
cookie we know today was not a Chinese creation but an American one,
a fact established in 1983. That's when real lawyers from San Francisco
and Los Angeles staged a mock fortune cookie trial at the made-up
Court of Historical Review. They settled bragging rights to the fortune
cookie's invention in the early 1900s, a time when both California
cities had proof of bakeries making them.

San Francisco won by a nose, based mainly on a letter from
George Hagiwara presented as evidence by a witness named Sally Osaki.
Hagiwara's grandfather Makoto was the landscape designer who
ran the Japanese Tea Garden in Golden Gate Park, where he introduced
the fortune cookie to the country, wrote Hagiwara, sometime
between 1910 and 1914. He even had the original cast-iron molds called
kata once used to make them one at a time.

That Sally Osaki was there to preserve the Hagiwaras' story
was maybe something of an accident: She was a Japanese American with
an interest in the history of Japanese culture in San Francisco, who
just happened to work for one of the politicians preparing the city's mock
defense. Osaki had gathered other letters, too, as well as more research
of her own. All of it pointed to the idea that the cookie was not so much an
invention but an immigration, an idea brought from rural Japan
to the West Coast.

PROOF CAME ALMOST TWO DECADES LATER, when
a Japanese historian and folklorist named Yasuko Nakamachi stumbled
onto *tsujiura sembei*, a traditional semisweet Japanese cookie that
came with a fortune. Until then, Nakamachi had thought fortune cookies
were Chinese, because she'd only ever seen them in New York.

The originals are larger, darker, less sweet, made with miso
and sesame rather than vanilla, and have a fortune tucked into a corner
rather than slipped inside, Nakamachi found, but they were otherwise
identical. She was so intrigued that she made *tsujiura sembei* the
focus of her academic research, tracking the centuries-old cookie's
transformation from a complementary "tea cake" served at Japanese tea
houses to its status as the modern symbol of Chinese American
food culture.

Tsujiura sembei first became associated with Chinese food, Nakamachi has written, in the chop suey houses of San Francisco. In the 1920s and 1930s, many were run by the Japanese. They served Chinese American food to Americans—chop suey being the trendiest such dish of the time—but also Japanese food to Japanese, Nakamachi's research shows. The fortune cookies were likely served free with tea or sake at these restaurants, Nakamachi believes, just as they were in Japan. By World War II, the practice had spread to Chinese-run restaurants, too. (You can see some of the menus of the time in Nakamachi's 2012 essay on the chop suey houses for Discover Nikkei, a website about Japanese diaspora culture.)

Golden Gate built a more automated version of their ovens in 2008, but it still requires maintenance. There used to be a company that fixed the machines, said Kevin Chan, but now he has to do it himself.

At Golden Gate cookies are still filled and folded by hand. They make ten thousand a day, said Kevin Chan, whose mother and uncle started the company.

IT'S UNLIKELY ANYONE IN AMERICA would have found out about Nakamachi's research if it weren't for journalist Jennifer 8. Lee. Lee followed much of the same trail for *The Fortune Cookie Chronicles*, her 2008 book about Chinese American food, eventually writing a profile of Nakamachi and her fortune cookie fieldwork for the *New York Times*.

As both Lee and Nakamachi discovered, the biggest shift for American *tsujiura sembei* came during World War II, when Japanese American bakers were essentially shut down by the government. After Japan attacked Pearl Harbor in 1941, Japanese Americans were forced from their businesses and homes, most shuttled to remote internment camps for the entirety of the war. Chinese Americans eventually took over the baking of the cookies; later, military men heading home from duty in the Pacific spread their popularity around the country, by asking their local Chinese chefs for the free sweets they'd seen in San Francisco.

By the time Japanese bakers could get back to their shops—after a Supreme Court decision ruled that their displacement was a serious breach of civil rights—a new fortune cookie history had taken shape.

ONE CONSEQUENCE OF LEE'S BOOK—which is as much about rethinking our preconceptions of Chinese culture in the Americas as it is about the fortune cookie—is its impact on Japanese Americans, some of whom are now reclaiming the cookie. One of those is Gary Ono, whose grandfather founded Benkyodo, a century-old pastry shop in San Francisco's Japantown that supplied the Golden Gate Park tea garden with *tsujiura sembei* until they were both shut down by the war.

Ono, in his own 2007 essay on fortune cookie history for Discover Nikkei's site, wrote of "childhood flashback images" of watching his grandfather's staff make them after they restarted the business in 1948. "I remember them being made with a huge carousel-like, heat spewing baking contraption," wrote Ono, who added that his grandfather had salvaged the first semiautomatic *tsujiura sembei* machines Benkyodo had to design to keep up with the tea garden demands.

Ono even provided a sketch of one of those ovens at work, drawn from his memories. They were dismantled decades ago, but it's still possible to get a glimpse of how they worked. You can either read Ono's story or make your way to Golden Gate in San Francisco, where something similar is still in use today.

HOW TO MAKE

GREEN GODDESS

CHOP THESE INGREDIENTS TOGETHER VERY FINE—LEAVES AND VERY TENDER STEMS FROM 3 SPRIGS PARSLEY, 1 GREEN ONION, 2 DOZEN FRESH TARRAGON LEAVES, 4 OR 5 ANCHOVIES. THEN MIX WITH THE ABOVE INGREDIENTS 1 HEAPING CUP MAYONNAISE, 2 TABLESPOONS WHITE WINE VINEGAR OR MORE TO TASTE, AND ½ BUNCH CHIVES FINELY CHOPPED. ALTERNATIVELY, PUT THESE SAME INGREDIENTS IN A BLENDER.

G

GREEN GODDESS

The history of Green Goddess is no mystery—the salad dressing
is the pride and joy of San Francisco's grand Palace Hotel, the oldest hotel
in that city. In 1923 their executive chef, Philipp Roemer, created it
from a mountain of fresh green herbs either for or in honor of a guest, the
actor George Arliss, who was in town to appear in a theater production
called *The Green Goddess*, apparently the *Hamilton* of its time.

What is surprising about this salad dressing is its color, which
almost certainly wasn't greenish in 1923, but white. Though the "original"
versions on record do vary slightly—there's one from the Palace Hotel
records, another sent by Chef Roemer's granddaughter to the *San
Francisco Chronicle* in 2010, and a few written up in 1920s newspapers—
in all of them Chef Roemer chopped everything by hand. He had to—the
blender wouldn't really be available for another decade.

And if you follow the recipe as written, as I did, you quickly
find that using a knife, a mezzaluna, or even a mortar and pestle instead
of a spinning blade will produce a wonderful flavor, but no more than
a few swimming speckles of green.

EARLY VERSIONS WERE GOOD ENOUGH THAT they probably
didn't need to be green. Though later sources often play fast and loose
with the ingredients, the three recipes listed above all included a chopped
mix of parsley, chives, and/or spring onion, fresh tarragon (usually),
plus a few anchovies, all blended with mayonnaise and/or sour cream
spiked with a little vinegar and/or lemon juice.

The recipe opposite—very close to the original with a little less mayo—is adapted
from one published by Duncan Hines in 1948. Before he became a cake mix, he was
a famous food writer.

GEORGE ARLISS

PHILIP ROEMER

I can attest that those ingredients in almost any proportion and any preparation—chopped, blended, Cuisinarted—are fantastic. Which fits with Roemer's reputation, too: In 1935 the book *San Francisco and the Golden Empire* called him "that famous Alsatian chef, one of the acknowledged leaders of his fraternity," meaning world-class chefs, most of whom then worked at hotels like the Palace.

ROEMER WAS ORIGINALLY FROM the town of Strasbourg, on the northeastern edge of France, near Germany, where a green sauce made with chopped green herbs, sour cream, and yogurt called *grüne Sosse* has been served over boiled vegetables and meats since the 1700s. That sauce was an adaptation of one made for even longer on the Italian peninsula, which probably stole it from somewhere between Turkey and the Middle East. The Italian version is made with olive oil, but, more importantly, with garlic and anchovies. If some of the appeal of the Goddess comes from a mountain of minced herbs, the rest comes from the whole anchovies—which appear to have been applied here before they became a part of the Caesar. There are also many mayonnaises from nineteenth-century France, flavored with herbs and countless other ingredients.

THE GARDEN COURT

Palace Hotel,
San Francisco

It is a testament to Roemer's skills that today his mixture of green herbs and small, salty fish screams California cuisine, even though it came together thirty years before that was a concept. (Side note: Many people trace its start to *Helen Brown's West Coast Cook Book* from 1952, which also included a recipe for Green Goddess dressing. It's pretty close to the original, and likely wasn't green either.)

According to the Green Goddess recipe supplied by Chef Roemer's granddaughter to the *San Francisco Chronicle*, he also pressed raw garlic into the curve of a wooden salad bowl before filling it with a mix of romaine, escarole, and chicory and topping it with the optional garnish of chilled cooked chicken, crab, or shrimp.

SUPER
GREEN

The first blender tech, originally created for soda fountains, was invented in 1922 by a Wisconsin engineer named Stephen Poplawski. It would take another decade and a half to go mainstream; push buttons like these came in the 1960s.

THE PALACE STILL SERVES what is essentially that dish as their Signature Crab Salad with Toybox cherry tomatoes and English cucumber in their Garden Court dining room, a city landmark with marble columns and pendulous chandeliers. The crab salad has actually been on the menu longer than the dressing, said Renée Roberts, who has been the hotel's press spokeswoman for twenty years and three chefs. In the early days it came with what was known as either Thousand Island or Russian dressing, depending on the year, said Roberts.

For as long as she has been there, Roberts admitted, the hotel has served what she termed "a lighter version" of Green Goddess, which is made by whizzing parsley, tarragon, chervil, fresh spinach, capers, garlic, shallots, sugar, anchovies, tarragon, white wine vinegar, Dijon mustard, egg yolks, and corn oil together in a blender.

They do serve a more historically accurate version on a simple salad of local butter lettuce at the Wayfare Tavern, which opened in downtown San Francisco not far from the Palace in 2010. It's the version from Roemer's granddaughter, said Tony Martell, the restaurant's director of operations, which was given to Tyler Florence, the restaurant's chef-owner. Though given the dressing's suspiciously green hue, I suspect his kitchen crew isn't chopping their herbs by hand.

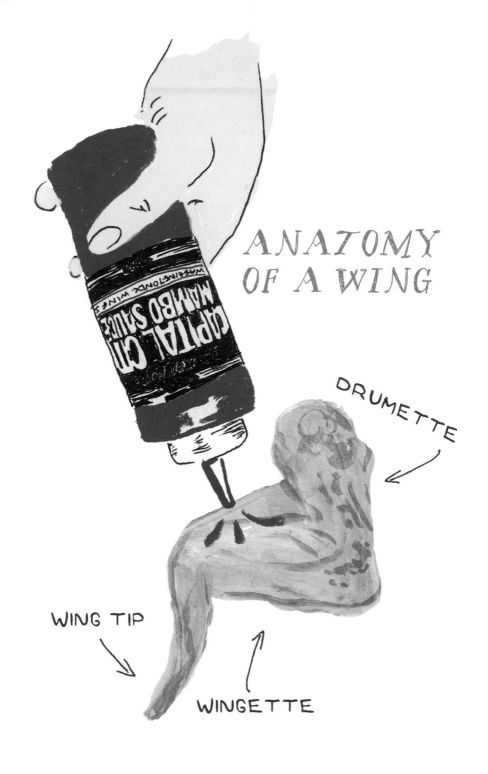

ANATOMY
OF A WING

DRUMETTE

WING TIP

WINGETTE

HOT WINGS

"Tourists Eat Wings. Buffalonians Eat Subs." So proclaimed a recent headline in a national food magazine.

Which can't possibly be true, unless literally everyone I saw on a recent trip to the western New York city was a tourist, including tables of high school students, old Irish American ladies at an old Irish American pub, people getting takeout at two A.M., and young professionals in their Bills jerseys mingling at a gastropub after a game.

Buffalonians may be the creators of much more than wings—they have their own pizza (somewhere between Chicago and Detroit style), plus stuffed banana peppers and beef on weck, to name but a few. But like Americans around the country at restaurants high and low, they love wings. They eat Buffalo-style hot wings, yes, but also wings grilled, smoked, suicidally hot, slathered with Cajun spice, and covered with various sauces. They eat them at the multiple locations of Duff's and line up at Gabriel's Gate and Gene McCarthy's Old First Ward Brewing Company and at La Nova pizzeria, which even has a national frozen wing distribution division, and countless other places that constantly make best-of lists and wing trail maps.

But they don't eat them battered and deep-fried and covered with mombo sauce at John Young's Wings and Things, gone since the 1980s.

THIS IS IMPORTANT because John Young, who died in 1998, had said it was he who started off the whole wing thing in Buffalo, not Teressa Bellissimo of the Anchor Bar, which now has a location in New York City's Times Square. And I think the story of John Young—who grew

---

DC mambo sauce plays an important role in the time-space continuum of hot wings—the proper name for Buffalo wings outside their native territory. (Buffalonians just call them wings.) If you want to try it, Capital City ships nationwide.

up with thirteen siblings on a four-acre Alabama truck farm, worked with his father on a riverboat kitchen, and moved to Buffalo for work in the 1950s with plenty of other blacks during the Great Migration—definitely has some credence.

No matter what happened, the Anchor Bar's Teressa Bellissimo is the creator of what non-Buffalonians call the Buffalo wing: It's cut into pieces, paired with celery and blue cheese, and, most important, has the Buffalo wing flavor, which today is a base of Frank's RedHot sauce and butter. As several have already pointed out, that is no small thing. (Including Arthur Bovino, who covers both the nationwide embrace of buffalo flavor and John Young in his 2018 book *Buffalo Everything*.)

John Young's wings were similar but different: Like the others, they were fried and paired with a Day-Glo reddish sauce he called mombo, but they were served whole and fried Southern-style with a crispy "Golden Dip" batter.

In 1996, Young told *Buffalo News* food critic Janice Okun that he served fried wings without sauce at several Buffalo restaurants he'd run since 1961—along with other soul foods like ribs and grits. After he heard about a fried wing place in Washington, DC, from a traveling boxer, he added the sauce and named a new operation at Jefferson and Utica Streets John Young's Wings and Things.

"The day we opened, people fell out of the sky," Young told Okun. "I was selling ten wings—whole—for $1 then, and people were lined up around the corner like they were going to a rummage sale."

YOUNG DIDN'T GIVE DETAILS, but we can be pretty sure mombo sauce was not totally his invention, though his recipe likely was. Since at least 1962 and maybe the late 1950s, there was a fried wing and "mambo" sauce place in Washington, DC, which was also called Wings N Things, and so popular it inspired the 1965 album from Johnny Hodges and Wild Bill Davis called *Wings & Things*.

By most accounts, the DC Wings N Things was inspired by Argia B's Mumbo Sauce, a barbecue sauce created by Argia B. Collins at his Chicago restaurants in the 1950s. He moved up to Chicago from Mississippi, where a mild tomato-based barbecue sauce is common. Collins's customers at his many restaurants put it on everything he served, including fried chicken.

TERESSA BELISSIMO

JOHN YOUNG

THE KING & QUEEN OF WINGS

In fact, an Argia B's–like sauce just called "mild sauce" has been served in South Chicago fried chicken joints since at least the 1960s. It's more like barbecue sauce with a bit of sweetness, while DC mambo/mumbo/mumble sauce has a little more sweet-and-sour going for it. That's not surprising, considering who now makes it: primarily Chinese "carryouts," which took over the fried chicken business after the Washington, DC, riots of 1968, which actually claimed the original Wings N Things.

John Young's sauce seems like it may have been somewhere in between all of these. (By the way, in both DC and Chicago, the fried wings served with it are often battered.)

I have also found a 1963 ad for pit barbecue with mumbo sauce in what was titled the "negro section" of the *Montgomery Advertiser* in Alabama, which leads to me to think this sauce either existed in the South or made its way around the country thanks to Argia B.

AS SOUL FOOD HISTORIAN AND AUTHOR Adrian Miller and others have established, soul food is an American cuisine, rooted in some of the cooking practices of African Americans in the Deep South. These then moved across the country during the Great Migration with black

ARGIA B.

Southerners like John Young. Meaning, when John Young opened
a fried wing and mambo place, it was a little like an Egyptian guy in Philly
opening a halal chicken and rice cart after seeing one in New York.
It was already connected to who he was as a cook; he just got clued in to
a more successful way to market it.

As Miller says of John Young in his 2013 book *Soul Food: The
Surprising Story of an American Cuisine, One Plate at a Time*, hot fish,
or fried fish covered in hot sauce, was common in black-owned
Southern establishments, so "a chicken wing drowning in hot sauce,"
he wrote, "fits squarely within the soul food tradition."

OH, BUT WAIT, YOU SAY. John Young didn't fully wing it till
1966, which is two full years after the Bellissimos have always said they
created their own. But, as several others have pointed out, there's no
definitive proof of the Anchor Bar serving wings in 1964.

This point was first made by Calvin Trillin in his 1980 *New Yorker*
article on the history of Buffalo chicken wings, generally considered
to have both made Buffalo's wings a national thing and to have first
given John Young's creation story a public mention. (According to
research by Buffalo writer Steve Chichon, there's no written record of

56

Argia B.'s Chicago restaurants are gone but his bottled sauce lives on. Mumbo is trademarked, which is why Capital City uses mambo even though mumbo is common in both DC and Chicago. But Argia B. probably earned the name: It's been said that white store owners made it hard for him to sell sauce when he was alive.

the Bellissimos' wings until 1969, when a phone book listing includes "chicken wings." John Young's Wings and Things is in there, too.)

We do already know at least one Bellissimo stretched the truth, considering that Teressa's husband, Frank, and her son, Dominic, told different stories to reporters over the years, which also tended to highlight their own roles rather than Teressa's. Now all three of them have passed away, as has the general manager who eventually became the company co-owner with Dominic's widow. (On the other hand, I found the court filing for "Youngs Wings&Things" in the 1966 Erie County public records.)

By 1972, when the first big article came out about the Anchor Bar's wings in the *Buffalo News*, John Young had closed his restaurant and moved to Decatur, Illinois, to run a food truck serving soul food to factory workers. His daughter told a news reporter a few years later that the 1967 race riots in Buffalo had made him worry for the safety of his family.

I CAN'T HELP BUT NOTICE that in three 1970s stories in regional papers, Frank Bellissimo specifically refers to Teressa's sauce as a barbecue sauce—like the original mambo sauce—meaning that's what they thought they were making. (Given that both American barbecue sauce and hot sauce are African American creations—Adrian Miller's book is among those that offer plenty of proof—no matter what, the Bellissimos were inspired by black cooks.)

Oddly, the first story, from 1972, says that while other places fried the wings, at the Anchor Bar they were baked in a really high oven. You might wonder, as I did, what does this mean? Did they lie to protect their "secret" recipe? Make the wings differently back then? Some combination of the two?

Plus, John Young's Wings and Things was located at 1313 Jefferson Avenue, just a little over a mile away from the Anchor Bar. Plus, John

That's me! Eating wings at Gabriel's Gate in Buffalo.

Young's Wings 'n Things was said to be a hot spot for traveling musicians, and the Anchor Bar was a jazz club, meaning any number of people could have spread the gospel of wings from John Young or DC to the Bellissimos. (John Young's daughter told a researcher named Amy Kedron in 2014 that Frank Bellissimo occasionally came to their very nearby restaurant and their father went to his, but I don't know why John Young wouldn't have thought to mention that when he was still alive.)

BUT I BELIEVE THAT NONE OF THIS really matters in the long run, and not just because the Anchor Bar created the flavor called Buffalo. What really matters is that Young—and by association his siblings and children and grandchildren—could certainly be as much a part of the hot wing success story as the Bellissimos, even if he wasn't a part of their creation.

John Young's mombo wings could be part of the modern Buffalo wing story the same way almost every decent wing in the state is: the way the grilled wings at La Nova pizza are, the way the Cajun spice dry-rubbed wings at Gene McCarthy's Old First Ward Brewing Company are, the way even the mass-produced wings at Buffalo Wild Wings are.

This is what Buffalo native and economic development expert Amy Kedron was getting at in her Southwestern Law Review article about wings, which was called "Stock Symbols, Street Signs and Other Color Lines: Capital and Subjectivity in the New Dual Economy."

Kedron wrote that because John Young was black, he wasn't able to partake in any Buffalo wing boom. Instead, his business—right where the Buffalo race riots took place in 1967 and closed shortly thereafter— never found the footing or the funding it deserved. If John Young's story had been told even a tenth as often as the Bellissimos' was, Kedron wrote, his family also might be running an empire of restaurants and bottled sauces today.

Maybe it's not too late. By all accounts, John Young's daughter still knows how to make the mombo. Maybe some aspiring entrepreneur will read this or Arthur Bovino's book and help her get it back in circulation. Maybe John Young will rise from a culinary footnote back into the Buffalo chicken wing king he once was.

HOW TO EAT AN ITALIAN SANDWICH

...ANY WAY YOU WANT

I

ITALIAN SANDWICH

Italian sandwich does not mean a sandwich like you'd get in Italy, or the Maine Italian sandwich, though that is also an Italian sandwich. This is the big American sandwich, the one with all the toppings on a whole loaf of bread: the hoagie, the sub, the Dagwood, the grinder, the Zeppelin, the hero, the Philly cheesesteak, the Delaware Bobbie, the Chicago Italian beef, and even the Louisiana po'boy.

The po'boy? But weren't they invented by the French-Louisianan Martin brothers during the streetcar strike and given to all those poor boys? Well, actually, James Karst skewered that theory in the *Times Picayune*, in his 2017 story whose title pretty much gives you the gist: "If po-boys were invented in 1929, how was Louis Armstrong eating them a decade earlier?" Karst found ample evidence that "poor boys" were first served by Sicilian sandwich makers to blacks, including jazz musicians like Louis Armstrong. (Both groups, said Karst, "were anathema to the white press.")

Now there are also Irish po'boys (as in roast beef with "debris"), Cajun po'boys (also known as fried oyster or shrimp loaves), and super-meta banh mi po'boys, thanks to the Vietnamese who came to New Orleans and surrounding fishing communities in the 1970s. And in NYC you can get a gyro hero, which rhymes when you pronounce *gyro* the right way. The similarity between the two words is generally deemed to be a coincidence.

KARST'S PO'BOY REVELATIONS MAKE SENSE. In 1962, the famous (and well-traveled) twentieth-century food columnist Clementine Paddleford said, in her historical breakdown of "big sandwiches," that the hero had been invented about fifty years earlier by Italians in New Orleans, "a workman's lunch to be ordered from the local Italian grocer." R. W. Apple Jr., the famous (and well-traveled) twenty-first-century *New York Times* food columnist and political reporter, wrote in 2005 that Paddleford crafted "intensively researched articles" and was "matched as a regional-food pioneer only by James Beard." So she should know, right?

A 1963 article in the *Atlanta Constitution* gives more detail:

Some say the "poor boy" sandwich originated in Naples—in Italy where the crisp-crusted breads come slim and a yard long. Whole-loaf sandwiches in this country—dubbed submarines, Dagwoods, grinders or heros—have been traced to the waterfront of New Orleans in the roaring twenties when American jazz music was taking form and substance.

They may have come from Naples, home of the skinny *filone*, sometimes called *pane Napoletano*, though there's plenty of longish loaves in Italy, including multiple forms of *pane Siciliano*. But Italian Italians didn't make sandwiches like American Italians, back then.

As Mario Pei, an Italian-born professor of language at Columbia University, put it in his introduction to the 1950 American translation of Ada Boni's *The Talisman Italian Cook Book*: Italian workingmen "often carry a lunch consisting of half a loaf of good Italian bread plus a hunk of salame or a few vegetables." It's not really much of a mystery to make the jump from that to a sandwich. PS—Boni's *Il talismano della felicità* was translated by Pei's wife, Matilde, who also added in a few of her own recipes, though not one for good Italian bread.

SPEAKING OF BREAD, A DIGRESSION: Though many people complain about what happens to traditional foods from other countries when they become Americanized (see Pepperoni, page 109), I argue that in the case of Italian bread, Americanized loaves are better for big sandwiches. In cities where big sandwiches are deeply woven into the fabric of life—such as in the Philly–South Jersey area and southwestern Louisiana—the breads used are soft but resistant loaves with slightly crispy tops and good flavor (even the crappy ones).

They are not like their precursors in the Old Country. They do not tear your mouth, and they don't feel stale or crumbly after two hours on

SOUTH PHILLY STYLE

a shelf—that's a widespread problem with the average hero roll in New York City, which is much less proud of its big sandwiches than Philly is.

This, said Jonathan Deutsch, is possibly because the Philly-Jersey-Louisiana bakers tend to enrich their rolls in some fashion, with a fat, or milk powder, or egg, or even some dough-relaxer-type addition, which gives you the extra softness. Deutsch is a professor at the Drexel University Center for Food & Hospitality Management. He grew up outside Philadelphia, taught for many years in New York City, and helped reduce salt in institutionally made hoagie rolls for the state of Pennsylvania.

Deutsch explained that the best bakeries, like Sarcone's in South Philly, also tend to use a "sponge": The dough ferments a bit overnight, which adds flavor. He also noted that in all these areas, "where matters." As in, it's a big deal which bread you use—even if it's one of the same three bread bakers everyone uses—"and you include that in your menu-ing."

AND NOW, BACK TO THE HISTORY: The first Italian sandwich might actually have been the Maine Italian sandwich from Portland. According to family lore that is thus far difficult to prove or disprove, by 1903 Giovanni Amato was selling his family's loaves layered with ingredients to men working on and near the docks. (Today a Maine Italian from Amato's features ham, cheese, pickles, onions, tomatoes, peppers, and black olives.)

SO IN THE EARLY 1900S you had Italians making Italians on the northeastern waterfront of Maine, and Italians making po'boys on the southeastern waterfront in New Orleans. Maybe it's no surprise that by the late 1930s, you read about Italians making submarines near the docks in the middle, as in Delaware.

In a 1937 column in a Wilmington, Delaware, paper, Wilhelmina Syfrit said the hot dog "sandwich" was about to be usurped by the submarine: "This is a gigantic, and some think, artistic masterpiece of the culinary art," she enthused. (She also called it a "glamorous 'snack.'" Hee hee.) Two years later, Delaware reporter William P. Frank set out to get to the bottom of the name of the submarine sandwich. Not surprisingly, his Italian American sandwich maker said it came from an Italian American working on a submarine who taught him how to make it.

Some say the name *sub* was created in Connecticut during World War II, replacing the preexisting *grinder*, but dozens of Delaware sub mentions around this time seem to disprove that.

THE NEW YORK HERO WAS ALSO KICKING AROUND by then: In 1939 columnist Walter Winchell said the best thing to eat at Coney Island was "the Hero Sandwich (a loaf of Italian bread with ham and Swiss, American or Bel Paese cheese)." In 1954, the New York *Daily News* visited the boardwalk yet again, eating heroes "crammed to the ears with either veal and peppers, juicy meat balls or eggplant." Though my favorite reference is the 1940 Associated Press story, "Man Injured by Sandwich: Sam Kava was injured Friday by a 'hero' sandwich (peppers, eggs, half a loaf of Italian bread)."

Interestingly, many assign the creation of the name *hero* for a whole loaf sandwich to Clementine Paddleford sometime in the 1930s. But at that point she was mainly writing for the *New York Herald-Tribune*, a paper defunct since 1966 and not easily accessible.

LAST BUT NOT LEAST, there is the greater Philadelphia hoagie. Howard Robboy, a linguist who published two academic works on the Italian sandwich in the American dialect—and who lives just outside hoagie territory in the submarine land of New Jersey—is still the de facto Italian sandwich expert. He has said that up until the late 1930s,

MAKE YOUR LUNCH

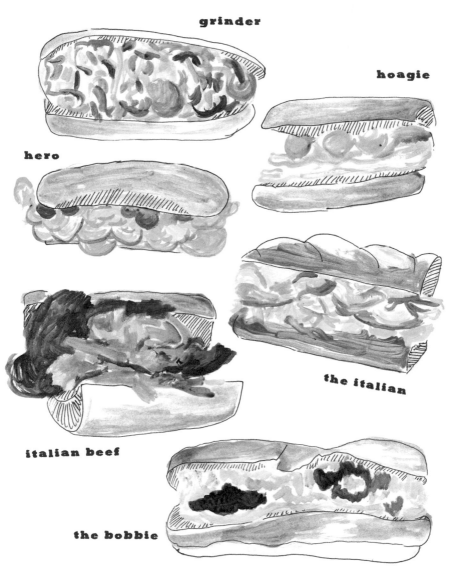

grinder

hoagie

hero

the italian

italian beef

the bobbie

SEE ALSO—
FRENCH DIP, CUBAN, PO' BOY,
DAGWOOD, MUFFULETTA

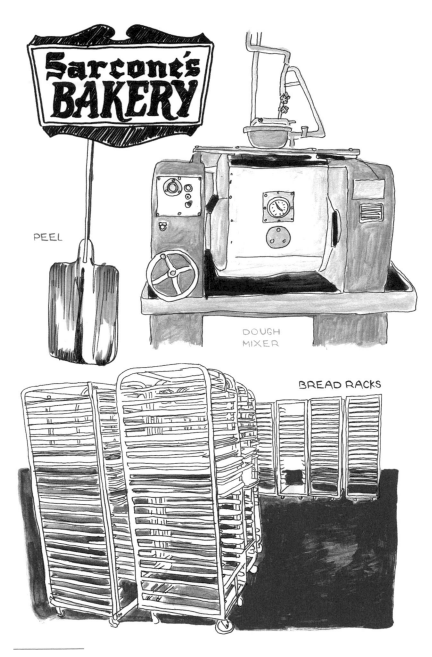

PEEL

DOUGH MIXER

BREAD RACKS

Philadelphia sandwich snobs know fifth-generation Sarcone's Bakery makes some of the city's best hoagie rolls. The coal-fired ovens installed just after they opened in 1918 have been retrofitted for modern use, but not much else has changed.

submarine sandwiches were what they were also called in South Jersey and Philadelphia. Like New Orleans, Philly was another waterfront city with plenty of Italians and jazz musicians, including one Al DePalma, who was both. He eventually opened a sandwich shop in 1928 or 1929, according to Robboy's research.

DePalma told Robboy that *hoagie* was originally *hoggie*, a name he created because he thought you had to be a hog to eat one. In fact, you can see *hoggie*, *hoggy*, *hogy*, and *hoagy* in Philadelphia newspaper ads even through the 1970s, usually in a classified ad selling a "successful steak and hoggie shop." (Steaks, short for cheesesteaks, are usually said to have been invented around 1930.) DePalma changed it to the spelling *hoagie*, Robboy told the Bridgewater, New Jersey, *Courier News* in 1971, because that was the way everyone was already pronouncing it.

Robboy's primary goal in writing his paper, by the way, was to show that the American language—and by association, our culture—wasn't collapsing into homogeneous conformity. He then proved it by compiling the broad array of names (and by association, beloved regional variations) for what is essentially the same whole-loaf sandwich.

On behalf of all big-sandwich lovers out there, I am happy to report he's still right.

RED'S HAM AND CHEESE HOAGIE
Serves at least 4 people

The best Italian sandwich ever, at least in my extensive tasting, was recommended by the crossing guard at Kim's daughter's elementary school. She suggested that we try Red's Hoagies & Groceries a few blocks away at the corner of South Ninth and Mifflin Streets. I had low expectations at first, given Red's half-bare shelves and unhurried air. But only until the counterman—a nephew of Red, so nicknamed because of his carrot top—made us the deli's favorite. That, he explained, was a ham and cheese with "pepper seeds"—or red chile seeds. I use a hot version of the finely chopped, whole pickled red cherry peppers sometimes sold as "hoagie spread." If you do not live in a place where good hoagie rolls are ubiquitous, go for a soft Italian or Cuban sandwich loaf. Err on the side of soft, not fancy. The one tricky ingredient is the hoagie spread. Worst-case scenario, buy whole pickled hot cherry peppers and give them a whiz in a blender or food processor.

1 whole hoagie, hero, or sub sandwich loaf	¼ pound (115 g) thinly sliced white American cheese
Mayonnaise	1 ripe tomato, thinly sliced (optional)
Hoagie spread (preferably hot)	
¼ pound (115 g) thinly sliced deli ham	½ white onion, shaved paper thin

1 Cut the loaf in half lengthwise, but leave it attached at one side so that it can be butterflied open.

2 Spread both cut sides of the bread with a healthy amount of mayonnaise. Spread the bottom side with a healthy amount of hoagie spread.

3 Place one layer of ham slices evenly across the whole butterflied loaf, then top them with one layer of cheese. The slices can overlap slightly— just make sure everything is covered. Arrange a single layer of tomato (if using) on the bottom side of the loaf, and layer on the onions. You want the onions to fully cover the opened loaf, which is why the slices should be as thin as possible. (You might not use all of your ham, cheese, or onions, depending on the length of your roll. Make another sandwich.)

4 Close the hoagie, cut it into thin slices party-sub style, and serve.

THE
JELL-O
GIRL

J

JELL-O

In 1997, on the hundredth anniversary of the invention of Jell-O, the Associated Press interviewed Martha Lapp Tabone of rural Le Roy, New York, whose grandfather Pearle Bixby Wait sold the recipe for $450 to "the wealthiest man in town," according to the article, just two years after inventing it.

Tabone, then a schoolteacher in the western New York State town of a few thousand, posed for a photo with a bemused smile, a Jell-O sweatshirt, and a fancy martini glass full of gelatin. She didn't seem to take the missed opportunity that hard: "I often say to our kids," she quipped, "just think, we could be rich and unhappy and living in the Bahamas."

IT'S A BITTERSWEET JOKE, considering that Jell-O, at that point doing a billion dollars in sales, has been hemorrhaging customers for a decade. Sales started to slump in 2009 and haven't yet recovered— as of this writing, Jell-O doesn't even have its own website: You just redirect to Kraftrecipes.com.

Luckily, in 1997 Kraft Foods had already donated fifty thousand dollars to the Le Roy Historical Society, which had earmarked the gift for its Jell-O Museum and Gallery. It's a super-cool place, a forty-minute museum of pop art and American culture and culinary history tucked in between the town history museum and its Little League field. It's just twenty-seven miles south of Rochester and half a mile south of the handsome brick factory where Orator Woodward, Jell-O's second owner, made the product famous.

Opposite: Many Jell-O ads were created by top illustrators. The Jell-O Girl was Rose O'Neill's creation and she appeared on every box between 1908 and 1949.

"You probably passed it on the way in," said a tour guide when I visited. "It's for sale," she said, "if you need a warehouse for anything."

You can learn a ton at the Jell-O Museum, but just in case you don't go, here's a short history as told to me: Unlike Pearle Wait, Orator Woodward was great at selling Jell-O. His Genesee Pure Food Company made Jell-O famous through clever branding and ad campaigns—the first of many to come, all captured in the Le Roy museum—and by sending out salesmen in horse-drawn wagons. They would drum up grocery orders and give out recipe books door-to-door. Orator died in 1906, his son renamed the company after Jell-O in 1923, and in 1925 it was acquired by the Postum Cereal Company of Michigan, then a part of General Foods.

THE JELL-O FACTORY moved to Delaware in 1964, and eventually, after a bunch of acquisitions and mergers I won't bore you with, it became the property of KraftHeinz.

Jell-O also added pudding in 1936, a product line whose twenty-year association with comedian/convicted felon Bill Cosby you can still ponder at the museum.

Jell-O's sales decline predated his, though, possibly because of a general shift in American dining habits toward the from-scratch, the organic, the rustic, and the DIY, not to mention an increase in fancy cupcake shops where you can buy your nostalgic sugar fix even more easily than you can boil water.

It didn't help that a slew of newish food history books don't do Jell-O any favors—like *Perfection Salad*, Laura Shapiro's hilarious academic work on the ridiculousness of the new "domestic science" promoted at the turn of the twentieth century. (The book was named after a lemon gelatin salad stuffed with vegetables and olives created by a Jell-O competitor called Knox.)

YET JELL-O HAS WEATHERED STORMS of consumer scorn before. Jane Snow, a food writer and syndicated columnist for the *Akron*

Opposite: Fancy molds, artistic ad campaigns like the "Jell-O Girl" on page 70, and door-to-door salesmen were a big part of Jell-O's initial success—though the salesmen schlepped recipe books, not actual Jell-O.

JELL-O

NEAPOLITAN JELL-O

DISSOLVE A PACKET OF LEMON JELL-O IN A PINT OF BOILING WATER. POUR 2/3 OF IT INTO A LOAF PAN MOLD, & WHEN IT HAS SET WHIP THE REST WITH A COUPLE OF TABLESPOONS OF HEAVY CREAM, POUR IT ON AND LET IT HARDEN TOO. DO THE SAME TO A PACKET OF STRAWBERRY OR RASPBERRY JELL-O TO MAKE A TOTAL OF FOUR LAYERS. ALL LAYERS MUST BE HARDENED BEFORE OTHERS ARE ADDED.

ROMAN SPONGE

DISSOLVE A PACKET OF CHERRY JELL-O IN A CUP OF BOILING WATER AND CHILL. AS SOON AS JELL-O IS COLD, WHIP TO CONSISTENCY OF WHIPPED CREAM. THEN ADD 1 CUP OF WHIPPED CREAM, ½ DOZEN FULLY CRUMBLED MACAROONS, AND A HANDFUL OF CHOPPED NUTS. SET AWAY TO HARDEN AND GARNISH WITH CHERRIES AND WHIPPED CREAM.

ADAPTED FROM JELL-O

The First Four Flavors

LEMON FLAVOR

STRAWBERRY FLAVOR

RASPBERRY FLAVOR

ORANGE FLAVOR

Beacon Journal in Ohio—the heart of the Jell-O Belt, a term she helped take nationwide—was there for one of them. You can envision her glee as she composed this line in 1985, heralding Jell-O's (temporary) return to popularity: "A backlash is brewing in the world of haute cuisine. After a decade of radicchio, goat cheese and sushi, a few bold folks are whispering, 'Enough.'"

Snow's topic was *Square Meals*, a cookbook by food writer Jane Stern and her husband, Michael, both experts on classic American comfort food. The book had an entire chapter on gelatin and possibly the first reference to the Belt, which Stern defined to Snow as "everything between Nebraska and Ohio." Today it would also include Utah or any other state with a large population of Mormons, whose religion imposes rules on food preparation and preparedness.

In the story, Stern told Snow she collected her Jell-O recipes after a TV appearance in Cleveland in 1983—there was a Jell-O competition on the same program.

Stern was smitten, and why not? Perfection salad aside, plenty of the old Jell-O gelatin recipes are genuinely good, like the two antique specimens we've reprinted here. I think it's totally true what Snow wrote about Jell-O desserts back in 1985: "Your sophisticated friends may sniff, but we bet they'll gobble them up."

MODERN KETCHUP DISPENSER

K

KETCHUP

The biggest shift in modern ketchup buying was put into motion in 2004, when *The New Yorker* told us it would never happen.

According to "The Ketchup Conundrum"—writer Malcolm Gladwell's famous contribution to that year's food issue—you couldn't create the Grey Poupon or chunky Ragú of ketchup, even though the mustard and red sauce categories were once narrow, too. The reason was that Heinz (and Hunt's and Del Monte, and a handful of other makers that had mastered ketchup's unique balance of salty, sour, sweet, and savory) was already perfect.

Gladwell's story became the inspiration for Mark Ramadan and Scott Norton, whose Sir Kensington's ketchup brand took form the next year, while they were students at Brown University. "That article was part of the research," Ramadan once told me. "We didn't believe it, basically."

By 2017 Sir Kensington's was so successful, Unilever bought the company.

REREAD GLADWELL'S ARTICLE TODAY, and it seems obvious that it wasn't consumers who were the problem, but the product. Gladwell had been tracking an alternative ketchup brand from Boston called World's Best. It was made with maple syrup and basil, and it sounds kind of terrible. (Had there been digital versions of stories enabled with comments at the time, that would likely have been pointed out by almost everyone.)

In truth, Sir Kensington's really uses the same approach and same theory of balance as Heinz and Hunt's. (That balance, Gladwell informs

---

Opposite: A modern-day ketchup dispenser, as seen at a Jack in the Box in San Jose, California

us, is known in the biz as "amplitude.") Sir Kensington's is just more thoughtfully sourced, as in whole tomatoes instead of all concentrate, and organic cane sugar instead of high-fructose corn syrup, and maybe it's seasoned a tiny bit differently and packaged with a mascot wearing a top hat and a monocle. (As Gladwell noted, Grey Poupon's success showed that Americans were willing to pay more "as long as what they were buying carried with it an air of sophistication and complex aromatics.")

Sir Kensington is also not the only competitor these days. Those slimly stocked ketchup shelves have grown to accommodate a dozen or more brands big and small that are following roughly the same "clean label" approach, including Heinz itself. The real appeal of most of these newcomers, I'd argue, isn't flavor but product purity, which is why Sir Kensington's is now crushing it with high-end versions of formerly pedestrian condiments like mayonnaise, ranch dressing, and honey mustard.

Despite its universal appeal, ketchup is endlessly disparaged as sacrilege on our most iconic food groups (hot dogs); while those who apply it with abandon are scorned by the food police as tasteless and tacky. Ketchup lovers, don't let them get you down: You obviously know perfection when you see it. Though it does have a lot of sugar, so be smart.

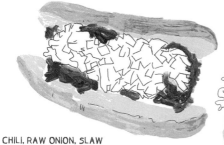

CHILI, RAW ONION, SLAW
—NORTH & SOUTH CAROLINA

CINNAMON-SPICED CHILI, RAW ONIONS,
SHREDDED CHEESE   —CINCINNATI

FRENCH FRIES, BBQ SAUCE, SLAW
—CLEVELAND

"NOBODY, I MEAN
NOBODY, PUTS
KETCHUP ON A HOT
DOG" —DIRTY HARRY

PEPPERS, ONIONS, POTATOES
—NEW JERSEY

MUSTARD, RELISH, RAW ONION,
PICKLES, SPORT PEPPERS,
TOMATOES, CELERY SALT
—CHICAGO

CREAM CHEESE, GRILLED ONIONS, JALAPEÑOS
—SEATTLE

OLDE KETCHUP RECIPE

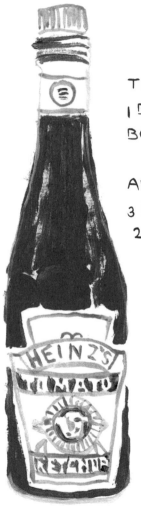

TAKE
1 BUSHEL TOMATOES
BOIL TILL SOFT
    & PUSH THROUGH SIEVE
ADD ½ GALLON VINEGAR
3 HALF PINTS SALT
2 OZ. CLOVES
  ¼ LB ALLSPICE
3 OZ. CAYENNE PEPPER
3 TABLESPOONFULS
    BLACK PEPPER
5 HEADS SKINNED
  & SEPARATED GARLIC
MIX & BOIL 3 HOURS
BOTTLE WITHOUT
    STRAINING

ADAPTED FROM SCIENTIFIC AMERICAN, VOLUME 3, NUMBER 51, 1848

IT WAS A SEMI-SIMILAR PURSUIT OF PURITY that brought us the original American ketchup in the first place. This most mainstream American of products (now disparaged for its sugar content and overapplication) actually has roots in an old-fashioned fermented-fish concoction called *ke-tsiap*. It was first adapted from Southeast Asian recipes by the British. The first ketchups, both in England and here, were also made from things like mushrooms or oysters, which, like tomatoes and fermented fish, have plenty of umami.

The tomato ketchup flavor we know today—with that sweet-tart pucker—was perfected in Pittsburgh by the Heinz family. The company started out selling produce and pickles from their Pennsylvania farm. Henry J. Heinz, by then already a successful businessman, was set on ridding the food supply of sodium benzoate, a preservative then used in many ketchups. He used his clout to help pass the Pure Food and Drugs Act, the precursor of the Food and Drug Administration, in 1906. He reworked his recipe in the process, packaging his ketchup in glass bottles labeled "guaranteed pure."

(The law increased consumer safety, many have noted, but may have also conveniently put some of his competitors out of business.)

New sodium benzoate–free ketchups had to be high in sugar, heavy on the vinegar and made with better-quality tomatoes in order to stay shelf-stable. The result? One hundred years of perfection, apparently.

The original ketchups were often strongly flavored. A century later, makers are finally making ketchup with some *picante* again, and spicy ketchups with chiles or sriracha are gaining a foothold. There's also the new Heinz "Mayochup," which, if you are from Utah or Puerto Rico, is already a well-established condiment category known as "fry sauce" or "mayo-ketchup," respectively.

L

LUNCHBOX

The Thermos came first. The vacuum-based insulated glass bottle had been patented by 1904, and lunchboxes to carry them in were the next step: American Thermos made a workingman's lunch kit in the early 1900s, and also one for kids. But it wasn't till the competitor Aladdin Industries licensed the rights to Hopalong Cassidy in 1050 (he was joined by nearly every other TV show or movie character for the next three decades) that the metal lunchbox became standard gear for every schoolkid in America.

The first iterations of the lunchbox, rather than the lunch pail or lunch basket or lunch-tied-up-in-a-handkerchief, began after the Industrial Revolution, when adults had to start carrying their lunch to work with them instead of eating it at home. The first were cast-off tobacco, tea, and cookie tins, some gussied up with homemade handles.

All versions are now collector's items—there's at least one of each in the Smithsonian National Museum of American History's exhibit on lunchboxes—but none have remained ingrained in the American psyche like the metal lunchbox, which continues to endure in pop culture long after it left the cafeteria.

THE COLLECTORS ARE OFTEN AS REMARKABLE as the collectible, when it comes to lunchboxes. You have Lee Garner, whose eloquently written *The Paileontologist's Retort* came out in the 1980s and '90s, a glossy little zine with photos of rare lunchboxes (like a 1957 Toppie the Elephant) and zippy essays from contributors like Jan Baker-Carlson,

---

Opposite: Antique lunchboxes. Today many modern ones are evaluated by Betty Gold, a kitchen product analyst for *Good Housekeeping*. They haven't put an old metal one through their temperature-controlled food safety tests, but Gold is pretty sure how it would perform: "terribly."

who penned "Memoirs of a Pailaholic's Wife." You have Scott Bruce, who wrote the hilariously named *Hot Boxing* newsletter, published two books on box collecting, and amassed and sold off a fortune's worth of lunchboxes himself, becoming semifamous in the process. (Amazingly, he claims to also be related to the Donut Captain on page 29.)

You have Allen Woodall, the curator of the Lunchbox Museum in Columbus, Georgia, who has thousands of boxes and as of this writing is still searching for a Toppie box. (Though he does have the thermos.) And you have D. J. Jayasekara, owner and founder of lunchbox.com, based in Pasadena, California, who sells new models of boxes but can custom-make you an oldie if you want.

One of the most romantic pieces of metal lunchbox ephemera I have found comes from Yance Wyatt, an associate professor of writing at the University of Southern California in Los Angeles. It is a wonderful short, semiautobiographical work from 2007 called "Lunchboxing." It's a blend of lunchbox history and the life story of Wyatt's father, a product designer and director of R&D for Aladdin over four decades.

In Wyatt's fictional recounting, his father helped spark the metal lunchbox's decline when he drafted the first-ever design for a plastic one in 1972, which was then nearly poached by a competitor after a lunchbox conference on New Year's Eve. In real life, said Wyatt, his father wasn't the one at the company responsible for creating the plastic box, but "he was very involved in the design of the first foam-insulated coffee mug. You might remember it; it had a handle and a snap-on lid with a hole for a straw."

LUNCHBOXES WOULD PROBABLY HAVE become something else anyway, given the rise of the school backpack in the 1980s. That was thanks to L.L.Bean on the East Coast and JanSport on the West, according to "From 'Book Strap' to 'Burrito': A History of the School Backpack," a 2015 story by NPR's Lee Hale. Backpacks just work better with something slimmer and squishier than a box, whether it's metal or plastic.

And so, the last metal box—it was Rambo—was released in 1985 by Thermos, who later brought a few back for a limited run in 1999. You can find new metal boxes now—Thermos has Mickey, and Aladdin has a red plaid "heritage kit"—but they're overshadowed by the dozens of other shapes and containers now available to transport your lunch. Thus far, none have become collectibles.

The Paileontologist's Retort, a full-color lunchbox zine that appeared in the 1980s and '90s, is possibly even more collectible than the lunchboxes it covers, given its rarity. You can occasionally spot one on eBay.

M

MONTEREY JACK

Depending on your point of view or your politics, you might subscribe to one of four theories as to who invented Monterey Jack cheese, all of which are detailed in essays preserved on the website of the Monterey County Historical Society in Central California:

1 It was Roman monks who taught cheese making to the Majorcan missionaries who founded the missions on what is now the central coast of California in the 1770s. (And who bulldozed over the native Rumsien and Esselen people to create a new Californio culture, but that's another story.)

2 It was Doña Juana Cota de Boronda, a Spanish-Mexican-German woman. Her family received the 6,625-acre Rancho Los Laureles in the Carmel Valley as part of the Mexican land grants from Spain, before California became a state. Her great-granddaughter wrote to the Monterey Historical Society about her father's memories of using a handmade jack to press the curds into cheese, then just called *queso del pais*, or country cheese. Doña Boronda, stories go, had to sell this cheese door-to-door to feed her fifteen children after her husband was injured.

3 It was a Swiss-Italian California dairy man named Domingo Pedrazzi, who also made a jack-pressed cheese in the late 1800s, which he sold under the name Del Monte Cheese.

4 But the most fun to tell by far is the tale of David Jacks, born David Jack in Scotland, who moved to California during the Gold Rush of the 1850s.

Opposite: Schoch Family Farmstead is looking to the past to cement its future. They now sell their milk and other dairy products—including the only Monterey Jack made in Monterey County—directly to local markets in the region. At Star Market in Salinas you can usually find everything they produce.

DAVID JACK

MONTEREY JACK

This Monterey Jack was developed by a Californian Scot, David Jacks, in 1882 — some say 1916 —. Monterey Jack has a buttery bland taste and melts easily. Quesadilla essential!

The synchronously named Jack (the man, not the press) didn't find precious metal, but he did eventually legally bamboozle the government out of thirty thousand acres of land, an acquisition that eventually enabled him to buy up most of the peninsula from Pebble Beach to Monterey's historic Mexican missions. That included many dairies making country cheese, including Dona Boronda's well-regarded *queso del pais*, which he started marketing and exporting around the country possibly on her behalf, probably with his name and "Monterey" on the boxes, so it eventually became known as Monterey Jack.

"THEY'RE ALL PROBABLY TRUE; it's not voilà—it's Monterey Jack," said Beau Schoch of Schoch Family Farmstead in Salinas, a third-generation California dairy farmer whose family is currently the only one making Monterey Jack in Monterey County. Like most who know the cheese's history, he believes it started out as a process—the time and temperature at which the milk ferments, the way you cut the curd to make a smoothly textured cheese, the jack that presses out the liquid—and that likely many people were making it.

"At some point, somebody said, 'Oh, what's this cheese? It's jacks cheese in Monterey,'" said Schoch, whose grandfather was a German-speaking Swiss dairyman who came to the United States in the 1920s to escape the flu then ravaging Europe.

Monterey Jack was once just simply jack, a simple, traditional cheese made across the region, like hoop cheese in the South.

NO MATTER YOUR TAKE ON THE PAST, Schoch is the standard-bearer of the future. It is an American travesty that most of us think of Jack cheese as the rubbery white squares sold in every supermarket. At its best—which is to say, as made by artisans like Schoch—it is a rich, buttery beauty that deserves its due as one of this country's first artisan cheeses, best eaten out of hand instead of melted on beans and burritos.

Several makers around the country do produce similar special versions, but Schoch is the only one to do so in its original terroir. This is hilly land just off Highway 101, land that has been grazing cattle since mission times, once a rancho owned by a Mexican land grant family by the name of Espinosa. (Their original adobe house was torn down by Schoch's grandfather, said Schoch, but one of Doña Boronda's still exists, if you want to see it.)

Cheese making is brand-new for Schoch's family, who produce both regular and aged Monterey Jack, plus many other artisan rounds of Schoch's own creation. For him it's part of a broader plan to stay in business, now that they often earn less than it costs to produce their milk if they sell it to national distributors. (He originally thought about growing grapes and making wine, till he realized his family already grew cows.) The Schochs also make Swiss-style stirred raw-milk yogurt and bottle some of their own milk to be sold at local grocery stores and food shops along with their cheeses.

Decades ago, there were three hundred to four hundred dairies in this area. Now there are just two or three. Schoch remembers when his family used to graze twice as many cows in the fields across the highway, before the area's huge fruit producers realized you could grow strawberries on those hills, too.

SCHOCH'S FAMILY LAND IS some the most valuable agricultural land in the country because of the cooling fogs, constant sun, and fertile soils. In fact, this land is known as the "salad bowl," home to much of the lettuce sold nationwide, as well as artichokes, strawberries, and cherries. In some ways, that's good for milk, yogurt, and cheeses. Schoch's cows, a mix of Holstein, brown Swiss, Swedish red, and Montpelier, get leftover unsold fresh lettuce when they're not eating his green grass. ("It's better greens than you're getting in New York City," Schoch told me.)

Today, their own labeled products are made from just 20 percent of the milk they produce, Schoch said, but he hopes to slowly grow the side business. Who knows? Maybe other Monterey County–area dairy producers will join him, making the region's past their future.

**NEW MEXICO
LANDSCAPE**

NEW MEXICAN RED AND GREEN CHILES

Most stories about New Mexican cuisine—and it is most definitely a distinct cuisine, as in a shared set of techniques, ingredients, and recipes—lead you to think it's some kind of Americanized Mexican food blended with a few old Spanish traditions and a handful of ingredients borrowed from the Native Americans.

But it's the reverse that's really true, said Freddie Bitsoie, the executive chef of the Mitsitam Native Foods Café at the National Museum of the American Indian in Washington, DC. "New Mexican food, in my opinion," said Bitsoie, "is all Native American food, with the exception of dairy."

Bitsoie is uniquely qualified to comment. In addition to the research he's done for his position at the Smithsonian institution, he is Diné Indian, also known as Navajo; he grew up on reservation lands in and around New Mexico; and he went to college in Albuquerque, home to New Mexican culinary icons like the Frontier Restaurant and the former tortilla factory called El Modelo Mexican Foods.

PART OF THE PROBLEM is the word *Mexico.* "That's what starts this whole conversation," said Bitsoie. "There is this perspective": These foods came from Mexico. It doesn't help that so many of New Mexico's cherished old restaurants—El Modelo, Perea's Tijuana Bar, found inside a two-hundred-year-old adobe tavern in Corrales—tend to have names that reinforce that fact. Most Americans don't think about who and what

Opposite: New Mexico is a land of rusty red vistas under perfect sunny skies, of high mountain peaks, plateaus and plains, of hot days and cool nights. Its original chiles were those that thrived in the region's cool, short growing season.

was here before, said Bitsoie: We see tortillas and beans and tamales and all those red chile *ristras* hanging up to dry, and our thoughts head south of the border.

Yet consider a New Mexican breakfast at Perea's, which sits just north of the dusty rose riverbed of the Rio Grande. You might order a few puffy corn tortillas, plus pink beans, hominy corn, and eggs swimming in a chile sauce whose brick-red color lands somewhere between crimson and maroon.

Though these things may not have been served together on the same plate a thousand years ago, all likely would have been eaten by Native Americans on both sides of what is now the US-Mexican border, along with rabbit stew with sweet roasted corn and dried beans, green corn tamales and blue corn pancakes, corn-squash pudding, wild spinach, duck eggs, bison, and pinon seeds. In fact, most of these foods have been here since at least 1000 BC, just as they have been in other parts of the Americas.

MOST OF US ALSO TEND TO FORGET that Spain was there too, said Bitsoie. And Spain's invasion of New Mexico in the 1500s—real settlement began around 1598, still years before the first colonists hit Virginia—was a very big deal for the foodways of the region.

When the Spanish came up from their colonies in Mexico, they brought cows, wheat, cooking techniques like frying in fat, grapes for the vineyards that have now been there for centuries, the domesticated lamb, Christian missionaries, and, one could argue, a sense of entitlement to the land and its people. They also brought foods and people from Mexico—including mestizos of both Spanish and indigenous origin.

WHAT THEY LIKELY DIDN'T BRING, said Danise Coon, was the first New Mexico chile. Most research, said Coon, who is a senior research specialist with New Mexico State University's Chile Pepper Institute in Las Cruces, shows it was already here.

The original chiles of this region, said Coon, were hot and thin-skinned and had round shoulders that tapered to a point. They likely originated from ancient trade routes between Pueblo natives and Toltecs living north of modern Mexico City, though birds dropping seeds may have played a role, too. Many of those early traded varieties, said Coon, are still found around the state's many Pueblos. These are known as "land race chiles," to set them apart from commercial cultivars. One of the more coveted is the Chimayo, still grown in the high hills of northern New Mexico near a town of the same name.

Though the ancient peoples of this region likely ate chiles fresh and green, as New Mexicans do today, said Coon, dried chiles were far more important. Unlike the versions grown now—big, milder, broad-shouldered types that can withstand being roasted still green in spinning metal bins in parking lots—the first chiles were thinner by necessity. They needed to be picked red and ripe in fall and then quickly dried before winter arrived—hung up in the same glorious red ristras tourists take home as wall art today. For months to come, red chiles could be ground into powder or reconstituted whole into earthy red chile sauces or brick-red venison stews.

THE MILDER, THICKER GREEN CHILES New Mexican farmers grow today—they are usually roasted, peeled, and chopped up with a little salt, garlic, and oil to form New Mexico's extra-chunky green chile sauce—began in the early twentieth century with a Mexican-born researcher named Fabián Garciá.

Garciá crossed seeds of the pasilla and poblano, which he brought up from Mexico, with the plants already growing in New Mexico, said Coon. "His New Mexico number 9," she said, "was the great-great-grandfather of today's NuMex cultivars like Heritage Big Jim and Sandia Select." It also became the Hatch—the most famous NuMex by far—grown since 1948 in a town of the same name.

Garciá created less hot, sturdier versions of chiles, said Coon, because "he wanted the gringo masses to eat them." It worked. As the number of gringos has grown in New Mexico—and technology allows you to can, freeze, dry, and process green chiles—it has surpassed the red in terms of mainstream American awareness, now applied to everything from potato chips to pizza to green chile chicken enchilada casserole, made with sour cream, flour tortillas, and condensed cream of chicken soup. Today red and green chiles are both the symbol of the state, as well as two of its biggest commercial crops.

The DogHouse Drive-In on old Route 66 in Albuquerque started selling foot-longs—split down the middle and served in their own special bun—in 1939. Along with burgers, fries, tater tots, and fritos, they still come dressed with red (or green) chile sauce plus onions and cheese.

NOT EVERYONE EMBRACES the chile as the symbol of their culinary history. In their 2016 cookbook, *The Pueblo Food Experience: Whole Foods of Our Ancestors*, Roxanne Swentzell and Patricia Perea set out a modern Pueblo diet based on pre-Spanish foods eaten by native Pueblan peoples. The book is rich with recipes, but not a single one for chiles, red or green.

Those, say the authors, were Mexican, brought to their land by Spain.

Swentzell and Perea join a growing number of native New Mexicans reconnecting to their traditions, and also distancing themselves from any adopted ones, said Freddie Bitsoie. They may see NuMex chiles, and Indian fry bread made from oil and white flour, and enchiladas dripping with creamy sauce as signs of their forced colonization, which started with the Spanish and continued under both Mexican and US governance.

Defining what counts as traditional is also a complicated mission. Early on, said Bitsoie, there were as many microregional native traditions as there were native groups. But as the Spanish and, later, the Americans forced many to move or consolidate in relocation camps, the cooking became more standardized, as new traditions formed over shared ingredients or forced ones, like the wheat flour and oil and processed soups given out by the government.

RISTRA

AT THE DOGHOUSE,
A POT OF RED CHILE
SAUCE SIMMERS ON
THE STOVE AT ALL
TIMES, READY FOR NEW
MEXICO-STYLE HOT DOGS
AND HAMBURGERS.

CHILES HANG
TO DRY

The red and green chile tradition extends south through Mexico and north through Colorado along Interstate 25, which coincidentally runs along the valley where chiles grow well. Not far from its path you'll find El Paso, home to its own long chile traditions; Las Cruces, home to the chile institute; the New Mexican towns of Hatch and Chimayo and the Coloradan town of Pueblo, all home to famous chiles of the same names; as well as Taco House in Denver, Colorado, where almost everything is doused in red or green chile.

While the Spanish and later the Americans tried to forcibly change—if not erase—many parts of native culture, said Bitsoie, sometimes with food it was a fair exchange, as in desirable ingredients or techniques borrowed, learned, traded, and adopted.

Not to mention the idea that many New Mexicans today are themselves a blend of genetics: Mexican, Spanish, Native American, English, and so on. (Some more than they previously thought: A 2018 *New York Times* story about genetic testing reported that many New Mexicans of Hispanic origin have found out they have Native heritage, too.)

THAT BLENDED CULTURE IS found at the state's Indian Pueblo Cultural Center, where the café serves fry bread tacos with ground beef and red and green chile sauce in addition to bison short ribs with mashed yucca and agave-syrup-roasted acorn squash. It shows up at Chaco Grill inside the Shell gas station in remote Cuba, New Mexico, where you can order either fried sopaipillas or fry bread with green or red chile sauce twice as hot as in any found in Albuquerque. It shows up at the Golden Crown Panaderia just outside of Albuquerque's Old Town, where you can order cinnamon-sugar-dusted blue corn biscochitos and soft loaves of green chile bread. And it's found in homes all over New Mexico, in chile-loaded casseroles with sour cream, canned soup, and yellow cheese.

None of those things are completely indigenous or traditional to anybody, said Bitsoie, but once they become a part of your consciousness, your go-to comfort food, he said, they become a part of who you are. Which is why chiles mean home to any New Mexican, he said, no matter where in the state they grew up.

As proof, Bitsoie tells the story of the green chile cheeseburger served at the Blake's Lottaburger in Window Rock, Arizona, right on the border of New Mexico. "The Arizona people get jalapeño," he said, "and New Mexico people get green chile."

These jars were part of an exhibit titled "Grandma's Kitchen" at the Indian Pueblo Cultural Center in Albuquerque: "Grandma's kitchen contains both the old and the new, but one thing remains constant: The love and comfort that we feel while we are there."

NEW MEXICAN RED CHILE SAUCE
Makes about 2 cups

This recipe is based on one in the 1977 edition of the Pueblo Indian Cookbook, a little booklet first produced in 1972 by the Museum of New Mexico Press. You can add this sauce to stews, serve it on eggs, or make simple New Mexico enchiladas—which are stacked, not rolled. Put a toasted corn tortilla in a pie plate, top it with a teaspoon or two of grated onion and a teaspoon or two of grated cheese, then a little red chile sauce, then another tortilla. Repeat the process, topping the stack with sauce and cheese, then broil for a minute or two. You will have enough sauce for at least two stacks.

2 tablespoons fat or oil

1 small white onion, diced

1 clove garlic, sliced and mashed with a fork

6 tablespoons New Mexican red chile powder*

1 tablespoon all-purpose flour

½ teaspoon salt

Pinch of dried oregano

2 to 3 cups stock or water

Heat the fat or oil in a small saucepan over medium heat. Add the onion and cook, stirring for 1 minute. Add the garlic and cook for 1 minute, stirring constantly so that the garlic and onion don't brown. Stir in the chile, flour, salt, and oregano, then add 2 cups stock or water, stirring until there are no lumps. Cook at a low simmer for 20 minutes, stirring often. Add a little stock or water as needed at the end of the cooking process so that the sauce is the consistency of a thin gravy.

*You can also use 1 cup rehydrated New Mexican chile pulp and add just 1 cup water. To make pulp, wash 12 large dried chiles and remove the stems and seeds. Cover with water in a small pot and bring to a boil. Cover the pot, turn off the heat, and let the chiles sit for 1 hour or until rehydrated. You can then just puree the chiles in a blender with enough cooking liquid to cover, or go the messier route and squeeze the pulp from the skins with your hands.

———————

The Chaco Grill, technically a lunch counter in a gas station at the edge of Navajo and Jicarillo Apache nation lands, has some of the best (and hottest) chile that I tasted in New Mexico.

CHILE SAUCES OF THE SOUTHWEST

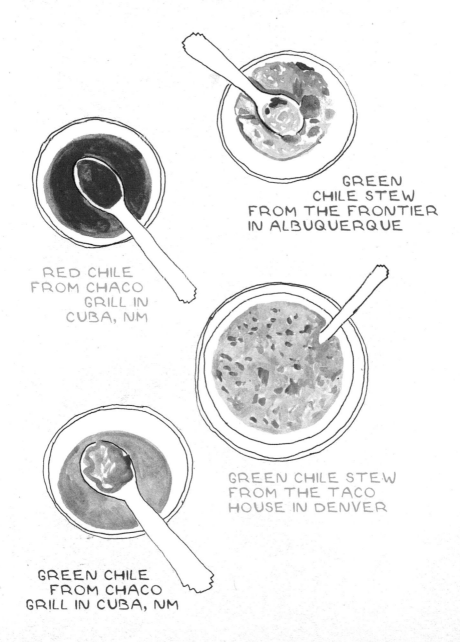

GREEN
CHILE STEW
FROM THE FRONTIER
IN ALBUQUERQUE

RED CHILE
FROM CHACO
GRILL IN
CUBA, NM

GREEN CHILE STEW
FROM THE TACO
HOUSE IN DENVER

GREEN CHILE
FROM CHACO
GRILL IN CUBA, NM

O

ORANGE JULIUS

I think the real Julius Freed—as in Orange Julius—may have been a cigar shop owner named Julius Fried from Butte, Montana, at least according to a 1983 story in the *Standard*, the local paper. If that's true, then he likely moved (fled?) to Los Angeles after bankruptcy and a couple of arrests for ignoring (encouraging?) the illegal gambling that took place in the back of his flagship store.

Which is funny, though finding the real Freed isn't that important. Freed did open an orange juice stand at 820 South Broadway in downtown Los Angeles in 1926, when those were common in Southern California. But it was his real estate agent, Willard (Bill) Hamlin, who made it Orange Julius.

Hamlin convinced Freed to carry his secret powdered formula that turns blended orange juice, sugar syrup, and crushed ice into that sherbety, Creamsicle-y goodness. He then invested $6,800 and went into business with Freed and a building contractor named William Larkin.

ACCORDING TO HIS 1987 *LA TIMES* OBITUARY, Hamlin had both a sensitive stomach and an interest in chemistry. In retrospect, his real estate background might have been equally important. As with Ray Kroc and the McDonald brothers some thirty years later, Hamlin seemed to predict the future: He and Larkin built beautiful freestanding stores with open counters in parking lots that could take advantage of the automobile, and sold hamburgers and hot dogs with names like the Mongrel and the Pickle Pooch. (He also added a then eyebrow-raising mascot with the tagline "A devilish good drink.")

Maybe Hamlin was more impressive than Ray Kroc, if you consider that Kroc didn't also invent the McDonald's way of making a hamburger.

When Hamlin retired in 1967 and sold the company to International Industries Inc., there were already more than four hundred Orange Julius outlets around the country, plus Canada, Japan, China, Puerto Rico, and several countries in Southeast Asia.

QUESTION ANY ORANGE JULIUS FREAK—they usually grew up west of the Rockies—and you'll find that it was not just a flavor, but a place. In 1931 in Texas, fans would have followed the ad in the *Kerrville Mountain Sun* and gone to "see it made on the new Sunkist extractor." In the 1960s they'd have hung out in the parking lot at the cool zigzag-roofed structures Hamlin and Larkin built across Southern California. And in the 1980s, they would have gone to the mall.

The mall years were great, but they were the beginning of Orange Julius's decline, at least as a destination. Eventually the shops stopped fresh squeezing oranges: When your product becomes a powder, juice from a box, and a sugar syrup, you don't need a whole store to make it . . . which is why it was maybe no surprise that Dairy Queen, after buying the company in 1987, eventually started combining the stores.

By 2018 all the Orange Juliuses had essentially become Dairy Queens, the only thing left of the brand being a few items on the beverage menu and a logo on a cup. (I think I may have spotted the only freestanding Orange Julius left while passing through the Vancouver airport in early 2018, but since that's in Canada, maybe it doesn't count.)

I recently watched them make an Orange Julius at my local DQ Grill & Chill in Manhattan. There, it's a scoop, a glug, a whiz in a blender. It's maybe not a pretty sight for the die-hard Orange Julius fan, but at least it survives to sweeten another day.

In the 1960s, "Googie"-style drive-up Orange Julius stands were iconic in Southern California. The last operational stand in Los Angeles, most recently a defunct burger stand, was rejected in 2017 for landmark protection by the city, though the developer who bought the land will incorporate elements of the building into the new construction.

Orange Julius was aggressive in its expansion in the mid-twentieth century, and a primary feature was independence for its franchisees. In the 1940s Verna Lewis and her son Arthur (top right) became the first blacks to own a franchise, near the intersection of South Central and East Vernon Avenues in Los Angeles. Their photo behind the counter was preserved as part of a documentary work about city diversity in the 1940s.

BEST BURGER IN LA

LA BURGER

BREAKFAST ALL DAY

MALL MEMORIES

MY SISTER
AND I, GROWING
UP IN THE 80'S,
HAD THE COOL-
EST GRANDMA
EVER. IN FACT
HER TRUE AND
REAL FIRST
NAME WAS MARVEL.
WE ADORED HER AS THE MOST BEAUTIFUL AND
GENEROUS AND COOLEST GRANDMA AROUND. SHE
WOULD PICK US UP FROM SCHOOL TWICE A WEEK AND
TAKE US TO THE MOTHERSHIP—THE MALL. WE ALWAYS
MADE OUR WAY TO THE ORANGE JULIUS AND GRANDMA
MARVEL LET US GET WHATEVER WE WANTED. WE'D
SLURP THE MYSTERY IN THE CUPS, COMPARING HOOP
EARRINGS AND HEADBANDS AND ALL SEEMED RIGHT IN
THE WORLD IN THOSE PLASTIC CHAIRS AND STICKY
TABLES, PAPER CUPS IN HAND. —LAUREN, MINNESOTA

"...FROM THE STATION TO ORANGE JULIUS I BOUGHT A HOT DOG..."

"B-BOY BOUILLABAISSE"
—BEASTIE BOYS, 1989

I NEVER ACTUALLY HAD IT,
BUT KNEW OF IT BECAUSE
OF THE LAST SONG ON
PAUL'S BOUTIQUE.
—BILLY, PHILADELPHIA

According to a 1953 interview with Hamlin in the *Argus* newspaper in Covina, California, the secret for Orange Julius comprised "seven pure food powders." One of the best DIY recipes out there comes from Kristina Wolter, an Austin, Texas, food stylist who grew up in Northern California and worked at Orange Julius in the mall when they still squeezed fresh oranges. She posted her recipe at her blog GirlGoneGrits.com in 2012: It calls for egg white powder, vanilla powder, and milk powder, though that's only three powders. As one of her commenters mentioned, that seems awfully close to instant vanilla pudding mix. I found that if you puree the juice of 6 juice oranges plus 5 large ice cubes plus 2 teaspoons of the pudding mix, it's maybe even better than what they're currently serving at the Dairy Queen.

CHICAGO PIZZA

CALIFORNIA PIZZA

PEPER○ONI

ST. LOUIS PIZZA

DETROIT PIZZA

P
PEPPERONI

If anybody could help solve the origin story of pepperoni—the Italian-ish sausage born in the United States sometime around the turn of the nineteenth century—you'd think it'd be Patti Fortuna-Stannard, who co-owns Fortuna's Sausage in Sandgate, Vermont, with her husband, Paul.

The big debate about pepperoni has always been this: Was it ever made in Italy, or is it a fully American creation? The arguments against an Italian birth include its moistness and smokiness. The majority of Italian cured meats—your prosciutto, your soppressata—are rarely smoked and are usually hung to age and rustically ferment and dry over time, instead of being partially cooked and quickly packaged, as pepperoni is now. Pepperoni is also made with a mix of pork and beef and with paprika, all generally associated with eastern Europe, not Italy.

There's also its name. American companies were making Italian prosciutto and soppressata at the same time in American history that pepperoni arrived, and we called those *prosciutto* and *soppressata*. Why did we call this one *pepperoni*, a term unknown in Italy?

PATTI FORTUNA-STANNARD DOESN'T KNOW how the sausage got its name, but she does offer some insight into where it may have come from: southern Italy, just like her family. Fortuna-Stannard is the third generation of Fortunas to make Italian *salumi*, or air-dried sausages, which they sell mainly by mail order. It's a tradition that began when her newlywed grandparents moved from Pedivigliano in Calabria to the cold coast of New England in 1908. They joined four million others who came to the U.S.—mostly from rural southern Italy and Sicily—between 1870 and 1914.

For more than a century, Fortuna-Stannard's family has produced a southern Italian style of the dried sausage called soppressata; a fat-streaked coppa, made from whole muscle meat; and brilliant red-hot links of "Soupy," a Calabrian specialty similar to soppressata but more coarsely ground. It's fully loaded with black pepper and paprika, red chiles being the hallmark of Calabrian and much of southern Italy's cuisine. It is called Soupy not necessarily because that's what it was named in Italy, said Fortuna-Stannard, but because that's what her grandparents always said when somebody who didn't speak Italian asked what it was.

"People say it tastes just like a pepperoni," said Fortuna-Stannard, and it is close—maybe like an extra-spicy version. But she noted that her grandparents made sausage just for themselves that was even closer. Like a "typical old Italian," her grandmother kept it in her linen closet wrapped up in cloth. "They didn't call it a pepperoni," she said. "They just called it dried sausage."

A few years ago, Fortuna's decided to make a pepperoni in that style, adding a little hickory smoke flavor via the addition of smoked paprika. Unlike most mass-produced pepperoni, it is fully dried and cured, rather than cooked and slightly moist, and packed into a casings made from pork intestines rather than one made of collagen or fiber. Today, said Fortuna-Stannard, is their second biggest seller after the Soupy.

A FEW RANDOM HISTORICAL FACTS ABOUT PEPPERONI:

- *Pepperoni* has been a name used in the States since at least 1908, when it appeared in a list with a lot of other sausages available at American delicatessens as part of a story called "The Social History of the Sausage," in a magazine called *The Gateway*.
- *Pepperoni* with a double *p* doesn't exist in Italy, but *peperoni* does. In Italy, it usually means "sweet peppers," as opposed to "hot peppers," which would be *peperoncini*. Pepperoni sausages today are nearly always made with paprika, which is a dried powder made with red chiles that usually are far more peperoni than peperoncini, though it can be a blend of both. Though Calabrian red chile blends are generally considered to be hot, they usually often hover around medium spicy or even mildly spicy; and in fact Fortuna-Stannard told me she visited a sausage-maker in that region whose chile blend included a little of both sweet and hot peppers.
- Early on, there are references in English to pepperoni and peperoni, used both for chiles and for the sausage. Some people used to think the single *p*

was for the Italian pepper and the double *p* was for the sausage, but when you look through early newspapers, you see that wasn't totally true until the 1920s or so.

- A 1919 article in Virginia's *Richmond Times-Dispatch* about visiting an Italian shop mentions hanging racks of "sopressata, bari, coppa, caparola and the very popular caserta peperoni," and an accompanying photo shows that it is the same skinny shape that Patti Fortuna-Stannard's grandparents made and that was sold by Italians. It also shows that this peperoni, if not all of them, was maybe considered to be from Caserta, which is just north of Naples, which is not too far north of Calabria. (Notice just one *p* in *peperoni* and in *sopressata*.)

- We also know that early on, pepperoni wasn't smoked: Centuries-old technical manuals list it as an unsmoked sausage. And even smoky-tasting pepperoni today isn't usually smoked; it often just has smoky flavoring or smoked paprika added. And maybe it wasn't always so moist, either: By most historical accounts, pepperoni was more of a drier snacking sausage than a pizza topping until at least the 1950s— a heyday for food processing in general.

THUS IT'S POSSIBLE THAT THE SMOKINESS, as well as the addition of paprika and beef, and the higher moisture from some kind of shortcut mass-production cooking process, all came a little later on— possibly an addition from the large-scale meatpacking companies that have been the prime source for pepperoni for at least the past century.

Hormel, a German-American company, was already making traditional Italian-style sausages for national distribution by 1915, according to a nifty 1966 company history called *In Quest of Quality*, and plenty of other big Midwestern meatpackers like Armour may have been shipping them around the country before then. (Note: In many European countries, *paprika* is a more general term for chiles; they also sometimes use the word *peperoni*.)

It's also possible that pepperoni got its name the way Fortuna's Soupy did: It's what an Italian sausage-maker called it when somebody who didn't speak Italian pointed to a sausage made with lots of not-very-spicy chiles. It's *peperoni*.

Still, most Italian Italians—as well as many American Italians who have made a point to study their traditional foods—tend to distance themselves from any link* to pepperoni, preferring to believe it had to be some kind of whole-cloth creation from somebody from some other part of the world, like the eastern Europeans.

In fact, as a food consultant named Mattia G. Marino told me when I asked him about the sausage on a recent trip to Italy, some Italians believe it came from the Romanians. As Marino tells it, Romanian immigrants already ran butcher shops in cities where Italians were moving. Or at least, that's what he learned while in graduate school at the Italian University of Gastronomic Sciences.

MEANWHILE, IN OHIO . . . Like Patti Fortuna-Stannard, Darren Ezzo also has southern Italian grandparents who made Italian sausages. He's actually fourth generation, if you count the fresh sausages his great-grandfather made after moving from Campania, the region just north of Calabria, in the early 1900s. The family business began in Buffalo but eventually ended up in Columbus, Ohio, where it's been Ezzo Sausage Company since 1978. Darren Ezzo is one of the company's best salesmen, following the lead of his father, Bill, who early on scored an order for twenty thousand pounds of sausage from what was then a modest Ohio-based company called Domino's Pizza.

Today, said Ezzo, the company makes around seventy six-hundred-pound batches of five styles of pepperoni a day and sells them to distributors around the country. Their sausages usually end up at pizza shops focused on quality rather than price, said Ezzo. He told me he usually says that he is the "smallest of the big guys," which means, he estimated, that his family sold pepperoni to about half a percent of all the pizzerias in America, at most.

EZZO'S PEPPERONI-MAKING METHOD is somewhere between the mass production of Hormel's (which would be the biggest of the big guys) and the handmade, air-dried approach at Fortuna's. The Ezzos cook their sausages before drying them but use no preservatives and only whole cuts of meat—pork shoulder and cheeks—plus a little beef fat, smoked paprika, fennel, and garlic. It's a combination they've found to produce the best-tasting, best-performing pepperoni recipe, said Ezzo. They even make a skinny size similar to Fortuna's, which pizza industry old timers consider "Old World style."

(Ezzo Sausage Company is especially known in the biz for what is known as "cup and char" pepperoni, which is exactly what happens to the thick slices when you cook them in a blazing-hot pizza oven.)

Ezzo couldn't tell me how pepperoni got its name either, though he said he also recently saw a similar sausage on a trip to Italy. It was air-dried, skinny like the Old World style, and with a little more ground fennel flavor than his own. Made just north of Naples, not far from where his great-grandfather grew up, it was called *salsiccia napoletana*, or "sausage from Naples." Like Fortuna-Stannard, Ezzo is planning to start making it soon, which may—or may not—mean that after a century in America, pepperoni is finally coming full circle.*

---

*Pepperoni jokes. Get it?

QUESO IS THE GOLDEN CURRENCY OF HEAVEN ABOVE,
FLOWN DOWN TO US BY NUDE CHERUBS SO THAT WE
MIGHT FIND A SMALL PLOT OF HAPPINESS IN OUR LIFETIME.
— UNKNOWN TEXAS FOOD BLOGGER FROM THE
NOW-DEFUNCT SITE DISHOLA.COM

QUESO

You might assume, as I once did, that the birth of queso—short for *chiles con queso* or "chiles with cheese"—is the point when pasteurized processed cheese product (invented in 1918) combined with Ro-Tel diced tomatoes and green chiles (which came in 1943) to make a north of-the-border version of traditional Mexican melted cheese preparations like *queso fundido*.

But that's not really true, according to Texan cookbook author, writer, filmmaker, and chef Adán Medrano. For starters, we must let go of the idea that queso had to come north to get to Texas. It was already here, said Medrano. Up until the end of the Mexican-American War in 1848, he reminded me, much of South Texas *was* Mexico.

Most Americans tend to think of Mexican people as always moving over a border, he said, rather than a border moving over them. Medrano—who grew up both in the Mexican state of Coahuila and in South Texas—is the most vocal of a handful of historians and other researchers who remind us that the state is a piece of an older, larger region, one with its own culture and cuisine.

MEDRANO CALLS THIS TEXAS MEXICAN, and his 2014 cookbook, *Truly Texas Mexican*, is his manifesto. In it he describes a triangular wedge of land that today includes parts of Texas and Mexican states like Coahuila and Chihuahua. That triangle, Medrano said, was the home of Texas Mexican, which by his reckoning could be considered yet another of Mexico's many celebrated regional cuisines.

Texas Mexican, said Medrano, is not Tex-Mex, though they overlap. That was an "Anglo thing," he said, a term that found mainstream acceptance in the 1970s and 1980s, he said, for the Mexican-style food made for non-Mexicans since the 1940s. Texas Mexican, as his book defines it, is the "cuisine of and by the Mexican American community of Texas, whose ancestors are the Native Americans who first lived here over twelve thousand years ago."

Before there was a Mexico, said Medrano, there were indigenous communities like the Caddo, the Coahuiltecan, and the Karankawa. (While many of Medrano's *Truly Texas Mexican* recipes are rooted in foods from native traditions, we can be pretty sure chile con queso came after the arrival of the Spanish in the 1500s. They brought the cows, and the techniques for making cheese.)

Texas Mexican is the food still made in homes and restaurants on both sides of the Rio Grande, said Medrano. Texas Mexican is his food, the food his mother made for him growing up—including her version of chile con queso.

TEXAS MEXICAN CHILE CON QUESO, said Medrano, is much more about the chiles than the queso. The version his mother always made him was even simpler than the one he included in his cookbook. While Medrano added milk and a little Mexican crema to make it more like the expected dip, his mother stewed together long strips of roasted green chile, tomato, onion, and cheese. They ate it with tortillas and made it with American anaheims instead of more traditional poblanos, he added, "because poblanos were hard to get."

Sometimes, said Medrano, they even used processed yellow cheese. Many poor Mexican-American families did, he said, especially after the Depression when the government was giving out what he called "relief cheese." And they called the resulting queso, said Medrano, *"queso relief."*

White or yellow, Texas Mexican queso is usually a special-occasion thing, Medrano explained, not an iconic dish that symbolizes the cuisine. It took off among those of European descent, he guessed, because they love cheese. (He recalls making his version of chile con queso for a class in Amsterdam, when the only cheese available was so sharp it made the queso nearly inedible. To his surprise, said Medrano, his Dutch students loved it.)

Adán Medrano's work brings clarity to what Texas food writer Lisa Fain found in the research she did for her 2017 book *Queso!*, which includes many versions of queso, both regional and historical. She may

THE VELVEETA TIMELINE

Velveeta, according to a paper by the historical society of Monroe, the upstate New York town where it was created, was not originally a flavor but a technique for making a processed cheese, invented by Emil Frey around 1918. Frey, who was building on techniques already established in Switzerland a few years earlier, was a Swiss cheesemaker making German-style cheeses in upstate New York for Manhattan deli owners. (He also invented a stinky American cheese called Liederkranz.) Eventually Kraft, which was already making its own processed cheeses, ended up buying the name Velveeta. The best-quality "American cheese"—which, depending on how many types of cheeses it is made from, will either be labeled "American cheese product" or "pasteurized process American cheese product"—is mainly all cheese. But once you start adding in various other ingredients—dairy by-products, emulsifiers, oil—legally it becomes process cheese food, and then process cheese product, the most famous of the latter being Velveeta.

not fully state the shared history of south Texas and Mexico, but the connection is right there in her research, which begins with many references to green chiles stewed with cheese—*chiles verdes con queso*— on both sides of the Rio Grande.

Both in history and in the present, Fain also found that in some parts of South Texas and southern New Mexico, queso had more in common with what was found across the border, while the rest of the state relied on some kind of American cheese.

Medrano would surely tell her she found two American quesos because there are two American quesos: one Tex-Mex, and one Texas Mexican.

CASERA COOKING
AT A CHILI
STAND IN 1930'S
SAN ANTONIO

In the 1800s, Texas Mexican women ran outdoor stands in San Antonio selling *comida casera*, or home cooking. Their popularity among tourists laid the foundation for Tex-Mex restaurants today.

CHILES VERDES CON QUESO
Serves 2

In her 2017 book Queso! *Lisa Fain referred to an 1887 Spanish-language work on Mexican food called* La Cocinera Poblana. *Its short recipe for chiles stewed with cheese—simply called Chile Poblano—forms the foundation for the below. (If you want to make it more like Adán Medrano's, add some sliced, sauteed onions.) Testimonial: I was among the many Americans who would have sworn to you that the Ro-Tel/Velveeta version of queso was unimpeachable. I was wrong: This is so, so much better.*

3 roasted whole plum tomatoes*

2 tablespoons unsalted butter

4 roasted poblano chiles, skin and seeds removed, torn into strips

3 ounces Muenster or Monterey Jack cheese, cut into cubes

3 tablespoons whole milk

Salt

Warm tortillas or tortilla chips

1 Heat a skillet over medium heat and add the tomatoes, crushing them up completely with the back of a fork. Cook just until they begin to sizzle, then add the butter. Cook, stirring continuously, just until the butter melts.

2 Add the chiles, then the cheese, and lower the heat to medium. Cook, stirring continuously, just until the cheese melts and is incorporated into the chiles. Taste, season with salt, and transfer to a serving bowl. Eat immediately with tortillas or chips.

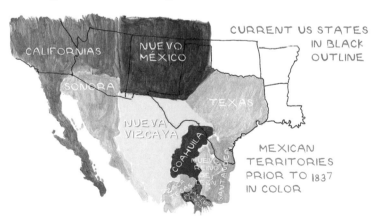

CURRENT US STATES IN BLACK OUTLINE

MEXICAN TERRITORIES PRIOR TO 1837 IN COLOR

*I usually roast the tomatoes and chiles at the same time in the broiler. The tomatoes are done when fully soft; the chiles, when fully charred.

APPALACHIAN MOUNTAINS

R

REDEYE GRAVY

In 1935, the Tennessee-born F. J. Lyle Shamrock schooled Texas readers of the *Amarillo Globe* on how to make a proper redeye gravy. It is "created, not made," he admonished. You had to choose a pig; feed it well; cure the meat for six weeks in salt, brown sugar, and cayenne pepper applied like a mother lovingly bathes her firstborn child; smoke it over hickory; hang it for a year; then cut a thick slice and roast it in the oven basted with honey and wine. Boil the drippings with water, he wrote, and then you had your gravy.

Tennessee—and the rest of the range of the Blue Ridge mountains— was not the original home of redeye gravy, but as Americans moved west from the Atlantic coast, it became its heart. Redeye gravy is made from country hams—the burlap-wrapped, smoky-sweet prosciutto of the South. The mountains are best for curing: They're cooler and less humid than the piedmonts of North Carolina and Virginia, where good country ham was born in the 1700s.

In the early colonial years, wrote Evan Jones in his 1975 book *American Food*, Virginia hams were good enough that Sir William Gooch, Virginia's royal governor, would send the ones made on his estate back to England. "Most of them were cured and smoked at a Tidewater settlement called Smithfield after the London market area, and soon hams bearing that name were being favorably compared with the long-famous hams of York, Westmoreland, Suffolk, and Bradhenham."

By the time Shamrock wrote his opus on redeye, country ham was often more about frugality than fine dining. This was poor-people food: Even if you raised and cured that ham yourself, you're not roasting a thick

---

Though found throughout the South, redeye gravy is emblematic of the Appalachian mountain region, where the climate and the culture is ideal for curing meat. The people there have long lived off the grid, making do with what they could raise, forage, or put by.

REDEYE
GRAVY

slice every morning, but frying up a thin piece in a skillet. And as anyone who has ever cooked real country ham knows, it always makes a sticky mess in the pan, so you add a little boiling water, or coffee, or Pepsi, and scrape up the little bits on the bottom.

THE STICKY MESS comes from how country ham is made: cured in seasoned salt for weeks, smoked for days, hung up and air-cured for a minimum of a few months and up to two years for aficionados. The longer a ham hangs, the more intense it becomes.

Across the South, most cure recipes are similar to the one writer Alfred Leland Crabb procured from the antebellum home of the Vance Brothers in Lebanon, Tennessee. It appeared in his 1966 paper "The Disappearing Smokehouse":

One large washing tub, 2/3 full of Ohio River salt
Add one pound of pulverized kyene pepper
One pound pulverized black pepper
Fifteen pounds brown sugar
Mix thoroughly

You mix the above with a half gallon of country sorghum and smear it over the ham. The fact that these recipes arose during Colonial times—when the enslaved provided both the labor to cure meat and the skill and recipes to do it—should be one clue as to who perfected country ham, according to culinary historian Michael Twitty.

As Twitty wrote in his 2017 book, *The Cooking Gene: A Journey Through African American Culinary History in the Old South*, "For generations the masters of these hams were enslaved men each said to possess a special savor to their particular 'cure.'" This continued after slavery too. (Twitty also noted the enslaved very likely didn't get any of the ham, just the fatty bacon.)

Even in Alfred Leland Crabb's story, which appeared in the magazine of the Tennessee Historical Society, African Americans were making the hams for white owners in the 1950s and 1960s. That's when ham making declined from a booming Southern industry to just a handful of mainstream makers. "I've just got one man left that I can depend on. That's Uncle Richard. If I had two or three more like him I'd have these beams sagging with hams," a Mr. Washington from Wessyngton plantation in Cedar Hill, Tennessee, told Crabb. By then, Crabb lamented, many of those other makers cut corners on both the cure and the smokehouse.

ARTISAN COUNTRY HAM MAKING HAS SINCE undergone a small revival, and as a result, so has redeye gravy. Like the best of the hams, it's now served around the country, served straight up on biscuits or grits as it always has been, made fancy with herbs and butter and fortified stock, prepared by all colors and classes. (Though as far as I can tell, all

REDEYE GRAVY

FRY A SLICE OF COUNTRY HAM IN A WELL-GREASED SKILLET UNTIL IT IS NICELY BROWNED ON BOTH SIDES. REMOVE THE HAM TO A PLATE AND ANY DRIPPINGS TO A BOWL. ADD ¼ CUP OF COFFEE, PEPSI, OR COCA-COLA AND COOK FOR ABOUT A MINUTE OVER MEDIUM-HIGH HEAT, SCRAPING ANY BROWN BITS ON THE BOTTOM OF THE SKILLET. ADD THIS TO THE DRIPPINGS IN THE BOWL, STIRRING IN A PINCH OR 2 OF BROWN SUGAR TO TASTE. SERVE WITH THE HAM OVER GRITS OR A SPLIT, WARM BISCUIT.

of the commercial producers of country ham today are still white-owned businesses.)

Plenty of cooks have traditionally added flour, brown sugar, and molasses or sorghum syrup, but I think anything else really takes away from the genius penny-pinching practicality of the original, where two breakfast items can be combined à la minute to give you a third.

NOW, WAIT, WHAT ABOUT THE NAME?

Some people say it came from President Andrew Jackson, who while he was a general in the army, told his hungover cook to make him some ham gravy as red as his eyes. As Jackson was kind of a racist jerk on all counts, and a chief architect of the Trail of Tears, I am pleased to say I am 99 percent certain that's bullshit, as you can trace that story to the 1965 cookbook *Bull Cook* by George Leonard Herter, which the *New York Times* called "a wild mix of recipes, unsourced claims and unhinged philosophy that went through at least 15 editions between 1960 and 1970."

Good redeye gravy begins with good country ham; the best are typically cured, hung to age, and smoked the old-fashioned way, though you can skip the last couple steps and still have a country ham.

If you've ever made redeye gravy, you also know it's not really red. Some recipes say to get the red you're supposed to strain off the fat and then add the coffee or water to the pan, then pour that into the strained grease. In a bowl, those separate into water surrounded by a slightly red ring of ham fat, thus the "red eye." But you don't really get any fat unless you add it to the pan first, and it still doesn't come out all that red, even when you use a ham cured with saltpeter or nitrate, which turns meat bright pink.

And here's another theory, which is that it isn't the gravy that is red but the ham. It occurred to me after I saw an old recipe called "red ham gravy" from 1917 and a photo of hand-cut country ham slices with gravy from some blogger in the UK, who had spent a year in Kentucky. Before the invention of the meat slicer, which cuts straight through the bone, and before you could buy smaller, skinny "biscuit slices," you had to separate the ham from the bone by hand. Yep, it left a hole right in the middle of that pink oval, and looked for all the world like a big red eye.

Andrew Jackson may have been a president and a Revolutionary War hero, but he was no friend to African or Native Americans. He likely wasn't the creator of the term "redeye gravy," either.

JERK!

SHRIMP AND THE RICE QUEEN

S

SHRIMP AND GRITS

Everybody knows shrimp and grits is a Low Country recipe, but that's only halfway right. It is a dish from the Gullah Geechee who live there, through and through.

The Low Country is a place: "It is literally low country: flat, semitropical, studded with live oaks, cypress, and pines, supple jack, smilax, and fragrant vines," wrote Kendra Hamilton in her 2007 essay "The Taste of the Sun: Okra Soup in the Geechee Tradition." "It's a land crisscrossed by meandering rivers, marshes teeming with wildlife, and now—since the building boom that followed Hurricane Hugo—crosshatched by mile upon mile of suburban sprawl belching forth the occasional town or multimillion-dollar resort development." Technically, she wrote, it's not just the coastal plains and sea islands of South Carolina and Georgia, or even Charleston, its cultural heart, but everything between North Carolina's Cape Fear and the mouth of the St. Johns River in Florida.

THE GULLAH GEECHEE, ON THE OTHER HAND, are a people. And their history began with the enslaved Africans in colonial South Carolina, who were brought there in the eighteenth and nineteenth centuries primarily to farm rice on plantations along the swampy coastline. Rice made the region rich—or, as the Charleston Museum more accurately says in its exhibit on Low Country history, it was "a kingdom of rice . . . built with blood, sweat, money, and thousands of lives."

Beginning in the 1700s, the enslaved came primarily from rice-growing regions of Africa, brought specifically for their rice-growing

---

Unique varieties of rice and shrimp were twin pillars of the colonial food supply in South Carolina. Today growers hope to replant old varieties like the hill rice brought to the Americas with enslaved Africans.

THE LOW COUNTRY

VERTAMAE
SMART-
GROSVENOR

Smart-Grosvenor's 1970
book *Vibration Cooking, or,
the Travel Notes of a Geechee
Girl* introduced the world
to the culture of her South
Carolina home.

knowledge. They came from modern-day Senegal, Gambia, Guinea-Bissau, Sierra Leone, Ghana, Congo, and Angola, as well as nearby Caribbean countries like Barbados, where they had often been working on colonial sugar plantations. By the end of the Civil War, they were among the first African Americans to gain their freedom, largely left alone on the swampy, mosquito-ridden coast.

People from these many different and distinct cultures lived and worked together in the Low Country, where they did the farming, and the cooking, and every task in between. They formed a new culture around shared words, traditions, and foods like okra and greens, seasoned rice dishes now called purloos, rice cooked with peas or beans now called Hoppin' John, red rice with tomato, pepper, and onion, or one-pot stews served with rice or thick porridges made of grain, including the native American dried ground corn that had already made its way to some parts of Africa.

"A common tradition could be built across vast linguistic divides" is how Michael Twitty put it in his 2017 book *The Cooking Gene: A Journey Through African American Culinary History in the Old South.* He was

talking about the unique Gullah Geechee language that also came out of
the Low Country, not the food, but you know what he meant. (Depending
on who is talking or where they're from, some people say they're Gullah;
some people say they're Geechee, hence the term Gullah Geechee.)

In South Carolina, diverse African traditions also merged with many
others, said Twitty: In the Low Country, the cuisines of Africa "joined
British, French Huguenot, and German foodways and the remnants of the
traditions of coastal Natives. Black cooks moved in and out of their own
comfort zone, creating their own cuisines based on flavors that might
be deemed too plebian for their slaveholders." And one of those was the
original shrimp and grits.

IF RIGHT ABOUT NOW YOU'RE WONDERING why shrimp over
grits became the most famous dish of the region, when rice was obviously
its queen, you're on the right track. Here's Twitty again: "Corn played
backup to rice in the Low Country and southern triangle of Louisiana.
Even in South Carolina, corn vied with rice as a staple, with one or both
starches starring in every meal." In fact, if you look at the traditional
names for this dish in Gullah homes and even high-society Charleston—
breakfast shrimp, shrimp and gravy, smuttered shrimp—you'll notice
what's missing is the word *grits*.

The original shrimp and grits might have been many things, but
it wasn't the recipe Craig Claiborne published in the *New York Times*
in 1985—though the article did make both the term and the dish
nationally famous, a must on nearly any Low Country menu of any kind.
Claiborne's recipe came from a white chef named Bill Neal who'd grown
up in South Carolina and spent some time in Charleston. Neal's recipe,
still served at Crook's Corner, the restaurant he opened in Chapel Hill,
North Carolina, had cheese in the grits and sliced mushrooms, bacon,
thyme, and lemon juice in the shrimp, and it required multiple skillets.

BUT SHRIMP AND GRITS HAS NEVER been "a dish for a white
tablecloth" in a Gullah Geechee home, said B. J. Dennis, a Gullah Geechee
chef who grew up just west of Charleston. Today he's a cook and caterer,
but also what you'd call an educator or ambassador—"whatever's clever
and sounds good," he told me.

SHRIMP
BOAT

Shrimp and grits is inherently a working person's dish, said Dennis, stripped down to basics, relying on the flavor of just a few ingredients, primarily the shrimp. It was sometimes just the small, sweet varieties rarely seen in seafood shops, he said, which were caught by casting nets in the region's tidal rivers and creeks. Those are often tossed with flour, salt, and pepper and sautéed in a skillet with some fat and a few slices of onion until the flour browns into an impromptu roux. Then you simmer it with a little water into a surprisingly satisfying gravy.

The finer details of execution depend on who you are and what you like, said Dennis: Sometimes the shrimp are cooked in butter, sometimes a little bacon grease or pork fat. Some cooks like heavily browned flour; some opt for just barely toasted, like the Cream of Wheat–colored version served with dozens of small shrimp at Robert's at Hannibal's Kitchen in Charleston's East Bay.

(P.S.: If you add okra and ginger instead of flour, it becomes a traditional late-summer/fall stew served over grits called okra and shrimp, with even stronger ties to African cooking. This is not considered part of the shrimp-and-grits family to Gullah Geechee cooks, but to my mind sure seems like a cousin, considering the okra thickens the stew just like the flour would.)

Note that at home any of these could just as easily be served over rice as grits or hominy, said Dennis, or even the millet or sorghum grains originally brought from Africa.

IN TWENTIETH-CENTURY CHARLESTON, according to Matt and Ted Lee, brothers who often write about the food culture of their native city, the early version of shrimp and grits in Charleston's white, upper class kitchens was also a simple dish. It was a one-skillet thing called breakfast shrimp.

The first written recipe for it that they found was in 1930, for a pound of peeled shrimp sautéed in four ounces of butter with salt and pepper and served over hot hominy. (This was the preferred Charleston term for grits up until fairly recently, hominy being the older, more nutritious form of grits, as it is made from nixtamalized corn.) It appeared in the book *200 Years of Charleston Cooking*, written by the wife of a former mayor who served in the early 1900s. "This is a delicious breakfast dish, served in almost every house in Charleston during the shrimp season," she wrote.

The recipe was from a Gullah Geechee man named William Deas, who was both a butler and a chef, and was the creator of other now-famous and fancy Charleston dishes like she-crab soup.

"MAYBE IT'S BREAKFAST SHRIMP IN CHARLESTON," said Sallie Ann Robinson, a Gullah Geechee chef with six generations of family on Daufuskie Island in South Carolina, "but here it's brown gravy." She has a strict interpretation of what shrimp and grits should be, and that is shrimp with a brown gravy made from toasting flour in oil to form a roux.

DAUFUSKIE ISLAND

Robinson refers to her own recipe as shrimp with brown gravy or smuttered shrimp—*smuttered* is "smothered," and this dish, made with sweet peppers, onions, and celery, is similar to the creole dishes made in Louisiana. Robinson included the recipe in her 2003 masterpiece, *Gullah Home Cooking the Daufuskie Way*, as Cooper River Smuttered Shrimp. The Cooper River is where she grew up fishing with her father for small creek shrimp—this was a dish they often had on Sunday mornings after doing just that.

To make her brown gravy, Robinson dredges the shrimp in flour and fries them in plenty of hot fat until they're brown. She pours off the extra oil, then adds chopped vegetables and a cup or two of water. This simmers together in the skillet, until the gravy thickens and darkens. Note that with this version of the dish—as with so many others in Gullah-Geechee cooking—you'll find parallels not just to creole cooking in Louisiana but also in the Caribbean, where they also make shrimp stew served over a cornmeal porridge called cou cou. Smuttered shrimp is the way everyone she knows on Daufuskie Island makes a shrimp and grits, said Robinson, "as far back as I know."

Not that they only serve it with grits, said Robinson: "You eat it with rice, eat it with sweet potato, you can eat it with stiff mashed potatoes."

CHEF BILL GREEN

SHRIMP AND GRAVY

Serves 4

This recipe is inspired both by Hannibal's Kitchen in Charleston and by Chef Bill Green of Gullah Grub on St. Helena Island, South Carolina. (Green, a respected chef, forager, hunter, and proponent of traditional vegetable-rich, seasonal Gullah cooking, makes this and other Gullah dishes in a series of YouTube videos that are a pleasure to watch.) Snobbier cooks might scorn the flour-and-water gravy, and the garlic powder, and the fact that the shrimp stay in the pan the entire time. Don't listen: The shrimp don't really overcook, the garlic powder helps with the browning, and this is delicious.

¼ cup (60 ml) cooking oil, pork fat, or bacon grease

¼ medium white onion, thinly sliced

Salt and black pepper

Garlic powder

½ pound (225 g) shrimp, peeled and deveined

¼ cup (30 g) all-purpose flour

Hot cooked grits or hominy (or rice) for serving

1 Heat the oil in a cast-iron skillet over medium-low heat. Add the onion slices, scattering them evenly over the bottom of the pan, and sprinkle on a little salt, pepper, and garlic powder. Cook, stirring occasionally, for a minute or two, just until they start to soften.

2 While the onion softens, put the shrimp in a mixing bowl with a hearty pinch each of salt and pepper. Add the flour and toss to mix.

3 Raise the heat to medium-high. Add the shrimp and most of the flour from the bowl to the pan. Stir occasionally for a minute or two, just until the shrimp start to turn pink and the flour starts to color.

4 Add enough water to the pan to come just up to the top of the shrimp. Cook, stirring almost continuously, until the gravy thickens slightly and the shrimp have curled. Taste, season with salt and pepper, and serve over hot grits, hominy, or rice.

T-BONE STEAK

The T-bone is the all-American steak, starting with its name, which is so quintessentially American: brawny and bold, straight to the point. Take the eighty-year-old T-Bone Diner in Queens, New York. Would it still be in business if it were called the Rib-eye? The Flank Steak? Not a chance.

An impressively large slab of meat crowned with a little scallop of spine, the T-bone looks like a steak should, too: 🥩 "It's the steak emoji," said Janice Schindler, a butcher at the Meat Hook butcher shop in Brooklyn, New York, where they cut down whole short loins into T-bones and porterhouses, the other fancy steak shaped like a T.

BOTH HAVE LONG BEEN CONSIDERED to be the very best steaks from the cow—big, fat-marbled, fancy beefsteaks cut from the short loin with one side of strip steak and one side of filet mignon, though the porterhouse is from the larger end of the loin. Thus it has a little more filet but also a tough nerve that meanders through the strip side. "Sure, by nature the filet is larger on the porterhouse, but at a cost of a less desirable strip steak," I was told by Pat LaFrieda, whose eponymous meat company is one of the best known in the country. (He prefers the T-bone to the porterhouse, so there's another point in its favor.)

Plus, the T-bone steak also sounds so much more egalitarian than the porterhouse, though in reality, the reverse is just as true. The porterhouse steak might sound like something from a posh London luncheon, but it got its name in America in the eighteenth or nineteenth century, possibly

---

Lucia Rodriguez made T-bone steak the lead item on her menu when she opened Mitla Cafe on Route 66 in San Bernardino, California, in 1937. (Incidentally, the Mexican-born Rodriguez was the original maker of the hard-shell taco—the founder of Taco Bell got the idea from her when he worked across the street.) Michael Montaño, the café's third-generation owner, when interviewed for a 2016 documentary about the restaurant, explained, "She wanted to have American food on the menu." To her, that was a T-bone.

from a beer hall (then called a porter house) or possibly from a hotel owned or run by a Mr. Porter. The word *T-bone* has probably been around a little longer, but "they are both," said PatLaFrieda, "usually priced about the same."

Whatever the origins of the terms, today the T-bone, not the porterhouse, is the American everyman and everywoman order. It's the fancy steak you can order at any corner diner at three A.M., albeit usually cut into slices about a quarter inch thick. A porterhouse, on the other hand, is usually at least three times as thick. (It's possible some of those diner T-bones are technically porterhouses. How would a diner know for sure? With a porterhouse, said Pat LaFreida, the filet must be two or three inches wide, while a T-bone filet should be nerve-free.)

JANICE FROM
THE MEAT HOOK

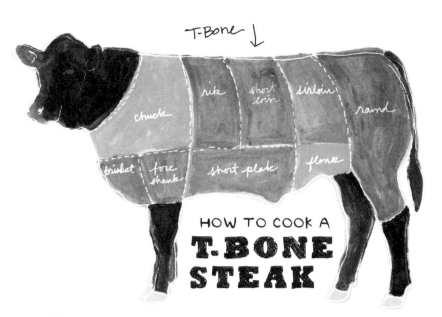

HOW TO COOK A
T.BONE STEAK

FRY IT UP WITH LOTS OF FRESHLY GROUND PEPPER AND FLAKY SEA SALT ON A HOT DRY PAN, SEAR IT ON THE OUTSIDE BUT LET IT STAY VERY RED ON THE INSIDE.

The short loin is the American name for a tender cut of beef that includes the top loin, the tenderloin, and some of the spine. Several steaks come from the short loin; the porterhouse has a little more tenderloin than the T-bone.

THE WAFFLE HOUSE is probably the reason for that, though it happened by accident. The twenty-four-hour Southern chain, whose menu proudly states that it serves more T-bones than anyone else in the world, put the T-bone on its menu in 1959. According to company history, a grill man at the original Waffle House in Avondale Estates, Georgia, got them from the grocery store when he ran out of the cut they originally served. It was so well received, they never switched back.

When the restaurant swapped in a rib-eye steak for the T-bone around 2012, customers revolted. And so management brought it back: "Based on overwhelming support of the T-bone, we have decided to keep it on our menu," said Vecus Miller, senior vice president of Waffle House, in a 2013 commercial. As the camera pans out to the kitchen crew, fans with signs saying things like I SAVED THE T-BONE cheer in the background.

Would they have rallied for the porterhouse? Not a chance.

UPSIDE-DOWN CAKE

U

UPSIDE-DOWN CAKE

On December 12, 1924, a Utah reader who called herself "Housewife" wrote to Kathleen Kaye of the *Salt Lake Telegram* looking for help with a recipe for a pineapple cake she'd had at a party. It was perfect and pretty and cooked upside down in a skillet right with its frosting, she said, but the hostess wouldn't share her recipe.

"I do not find such a recipe, Housewife," came the reply,

but can't you improvise? I've never seen this dish, but with a mind, a pair of hands, a skillet and the ingredients, why can't we make one anyway? I can't imagine the frosting going into the skillet first—or even at all, so I should proceed with the thought that we'll apply that after the baking. So, then, why not make a bed in the skillet of sugar and pineapple, then pour over it whatever sort of cake batter you prefer—rich, or plain—white or natural bake thoroughly, turn out while still hot, and frost, or serve plain with whipped cream? 'Fraid to try it? I wouldn't be.

And let's call it upside-down cake.

Welcome.

THIS COLUMN IS NOT THE ORIGIN of the classic upside-down cake—there are several recipes for it in newspapers around that year, plus one made with prunes, most of which were likely the creation of a twentieth-century test kitchen working on behalf of a fruit canning cooperative, or at least that's my educated guess. (In fact, that conversation between Ms. Kaye and Housewife might even have been dreamed up on their behalf.)

After pineapple packing cooperatives formed in Hawaii around 1907—this according to a 2007 article by Richard Hawkins called "The

Cooperative Marketing of Hawaiian Canned Pineapple, 1908–39"—they embraced the economic theory known as "contrived demand."

In other words, they made sure the American public wanted plenty of pineapple.

Hawkins, a professor at the University of Wolverhampton in England who is an expert on Hawaii's economic history, wrote that part of their plan included hiring salesmen and also plenty of price cuts. Those made sure Hawaiian pineapple was cheaper than the stuff from Taiwan or Barbados, whose tarter, tougher pineapples were the first to be canned in the late 1800s.

BUT MOST OF THEIR SUCCESS came from advertising, which targeted, Hawkins pointed out, the middle-class women with purchasing power. By the 1920s, when upside-down cake was taking off, those ads included not just fantastic advertorials in newspapers but the power of the place. Pineapple was a stand-in for the subtropical appeal of the "exotic," aka Hawaii itself, wrote Hawkins.

Cake making has changed considerably over the past several centuries with inventions of now mundane items like baking powder, created in 1843. Cake mix, which arrived around the 1930s, made upside-down-cake making even easier.

So was the pineapple upside-down cake. Though upside-down cake was and is made with almost any other fruit, it's only a classic with canned pineapple, whose perfect slices make it extremely easy to make a perfect cake. They were so well suited to the 1920s, when housewives were urged to make gelatin salads and neat food. (See Jell-O, page 71.) In 1925, after the Hawaiian Pineapple Company sponsored a contest for recipes, they ran an ad saying they'd received 2,500 submissions that were variations on pineapple upside-down cake. (Though it seems likely that HPC or another similar group had created the original recipe that inspired all of those.)

By 1930s, a little guide called "Recipes for the Use of Canned Foods in Cafeterias and Restaurants," from the Home Economics Division of the National Canners Association (compiled by Alice M. Child and Grace Erskine of the Food Research Laboratory of the University of

CARAMEL PINEAPPLE CAKE

A SKILLET CAKE · PUT 3 TABLESPOONS OF BUTTER AND A CUP OF BROWN SUGAR IN AN IRON FRYING PAN. LET IT SIMMER FOR A FEW MINUTES, THEN ADD SLICED CANNED PINEAPPLE JUST TO FIT PAN, 7 SLICES IS USUAL, 6 AROUND AND 1 IN THE MIDDLE.

THEN MAKE A BATTER OF 3 EGGS, 1½ CUPS OF SUGAR, ¼ CUP OF MILK, 1 TEASPOON VANILLA, A PINCH OF SALT, 1½ TEASPOONS BAKING POWDER, 1½ CUPS FLOUR. STIR AND POUR ONTO SKILLET. BAKE IN A 350° OVEN UNTIL DONE. QUICKLY INVERT ONTO A SERVING PLATE.

ADAPTED FROM THE CHICAGO EVENING AMERICAN COOK BOOK. PRODUCED IN THE 1920S, THIS EASY ONE-BOWL, NO-BUTTER BATTER RECIPE STILL WORKS VERY WELL, AND RESULTS IN A DENSE CAKE SIMILAR IN FLAVOR TO ANGEL FOOD.

Skillet cakes probably got their start in the colonial eras, when many Americans would've been using spiders, or footed iron skillets designed for an open fire. You can also use pineapple juice instead of milk, which makes for an even better cake, in my opinion.

Minnesota), included a recipe for upside-down cake using one six-pound can of pineapple that served 104 people.

Considering its audience was high schools, the military, large restaurant kitchens, hotels, and anyone else using canned food, it's not hard to figure out how a cake made with a fruit grown in only two states and indigenous to neither (it's originally from southern Brazil and Paraguay) could have become nostalgic comfort food for nearly everyone in America.

IT REMAINS SO TODAY, even though pineapples fresh or canned rarely come from the United States. By the end of the Second World War, Hawkins wrote, most Hawaii-based pineapple brands were so strong the owners found they could easily move the pineapple growing to other countries where labor was cheaper, without cutting prices or upsetting American customers.

It also meant that for the second time in the state's history, Hawaiian natural resources (its labor force being one of them) were used by commodity industries only until they found more financially rewarding options. The first time—as laid out by James Haley's *Captive Paradise: A History of Hawaii*—was for sugar,* which was refined in Hawaii up until 2017 after years of declines in production. (Like pineapples, sugar was squeezed by cheaper labor in other parts of the world.)

You can still support Hawaiian growers with an upside-down cake made with Hawaiian pineapples, though you won't find the fruits on the shelves in the US mainland. Instead get on the internet and find yourself a Maui Gold or a Hawaiian Crown, the only two commercial growers of pineapple left in the state at the time of this writing. Though you will have to cut out all those perfect circles by yourself.

---

*Sugar is one reason Hawai'i the island nation became Hawaii the state. In 1893 a group of Americans and sugar plantation owners—the sugar biz boomed in Hawai'i during the Civil War—overthrew Queen Lili'uokalani with help from the U.S. Marine Corps.

UPSiDE-DOWN
FRUiT

V

VINEGAR PIE

Vinegar pie may not be the most inventive of the desperation pies—known as make-do pies or poor man's pies, they're farmhouse desserts made from pantry staples and little else—but it is one of the most honest. Unlike so many of these desserts, which have been kicking around the country as long as we've made pie, it doesn't hide its purpose with sweeter names like sugar cream, miracle, mock apple (made with Ritz crackers), or Southern chess (made with cornmeal), the latter the inspiration for Milk Bar's registered trademark Crack Pie, with its sticky sugar-and-corn-flour filling.

Vinegar pie may not have as many addicts, but it's the special favorite of millions of little children (okay, girls) who fell hard for Laura Ingalls Wilder's Little House on the Prairie series. Wilder's books were set where Wilder grew up in Wisconsin, Missouri, Iowa, the Dakota Territory, Kansas, and Malone, a tiny town in New York just shy of the Canadian border.

In 1979, when the TV version was still going strong, Barbara Walker wrote *The Little House Cookbook*, offering a Wilder-era vinegar pie made of eggs, butter, flour, and sugar and seasoned with nutmeg and a little vinegar. "No display of holiday pies, whether on the home table or at a fair or social, was complete without this country standard, a monument to ingenuity and resourcefulness," wrote Walker. "Sometimes called 'poor man's pie,' it took the place of lemon pie in areas where lemons were as precious as gold. We think it would have been made this way in both Malone and Wisconsin, using both eggs and butter, but frequently the pie was made without even these simple luxuries."

Opposite: A little house on the prairie, where vinegar pies were once popular.

WHAT MANY DESPERATION PIES LOSE in fruit or other fresh fillings they make up for in sugar, or eggs, cream, and butterfat.

Take the heavy Hoosier Sugar Cream Pie, said Kate Scott, who fields many questions about this official state dessert at the Indiana Historical Society, where she works in reference services. It is ironic that with non-desperation desserts made with fruit, noted Scott, "you get a much lighter, less heavy pie."

In my 1987 copy of the *Pennsylvania Dutch Cookbook*, for example, there are many desperation pies, all of them variations on a pie made with lots of sugar or cream or both. There are vinegar pies, molasses pies, cottage cheese cream pies, milk and egg pies with white potatoes, sugar pies with the dried apples called schnitz, sugar pies with raisins, and brown-sugar butterscotch pies. There are desperation pies anywhere there are Pennsylvania Dutch, or Quakers, Mennonite, Shaker, Amish, and other agricultural communities, where eggs and dairy are plentiful. The Shakers and Amish, said Scott, also both make Hoosier-style sugar creams.

BUT DESPERATION PIES ARE REALLY EVERYWHERE. The Maui Extension Homemakers' Council of Hawaii, in their 1980 volume called *Our Golden Anniversary Favorite Recipes*, has the banana, coconut, papaya, and mango pies expected from the region, but also grated carrot, mock apple, and "impossible," which is a blended and baked mixture of Bisquick, sugar, eggs, vanilla, butter, milk, and shredded coconut, a pantry staple in Hawaii. (Impossible pies get their name because you don't make a crust—the browning edges do it for you.)

The 1969 *Cooking in Wyoming: Woman's Suffrage Centennial Edition* has a rum pie, buttermilk pie (my own family favorite), the aforementioned miracle pie (raisins, nuts, eggs, butter, sugar, and spices), and the "wonderfully rich" cream pie from Barbara Knighten of Big Piney. It's sugar, flour, cream, vanilla, and nutmeg, basically a Hoosier Sugar Cream.

Kate Scott's family might have made the most desperate pie of all, though, something they call "juice pie." Scott described it as a pie crust simply painted with fruit juice, a creation from her maternal great-grandmother. It's a far cry from the exceedingly rich desperation pies, which is probably a good thing, said Scott: "They're too sweet for me."

VINEGAR PIE

Makes one 10-inch (25-cm) pie

There are dozens of variations on vinegar pie: This one is my favorite, sticky-sweet and delicious, with a caramelized top. It works best in a pie crust that is just lightly browned instead of fully baked, and while it isn't traditional, it's maybe even better in a crust made of graham crackers.

4 large eggs, at room temperature, lightly beaten

1½ cups granulated sugar

½ cup (1 stick/113 g) unsalted butter, melted and cooled

3 tablespoons apple cider vinegar

1 teaspoon vanilla extract

1 prebaked 10-inch (25-cm) piecrust, cooled

1 Preheat the oven to 350°F (175°C). Whisk together the eggs, sugar, butter, vinegar, and vanilla extract in a large bowl until there are no lumps. Pour the mixture into the piecrust and bake for 50 minutes or until the top is golden brown and the center is set. (It will still be soft.)

2 Remove to a wire rack and cool completely, at least 2 hours, or refrigerate. This can be served cold or at room temperature and keeps in the refrigerator for several days.

HOW TO MAKE A
WHITE RUSSIAN

1 OZ EACH OF COFFEE LIQUEUR, VODKA & CREAM
POUR OVER ICE IN A SHORT GLASS & STIR

THE WHITE RUSSIAN

Fill a rocks glass with ice and add equal parts coffee liqueur, vodka, and cream, then stir, and you have a White Russian cocktail, a cocktail being a class of alcoholic drinks with the distinction of being an early nineteenth-century American creation.

Where did it come from? It may have had many parents: Years before the White Russian—which, by all accounts, first appeared in the mid-1960s—there was the Barbara (vodka, crème de cacao, cream) and the Russian (vodka, crème de cacao, gin). You also had the Alexander (cream, crème de cacao, gin or brandy), the Alexander the Great (vodka, crème de cacao, coffee liqueur, cream), the Russian Bear (vodka, crème de cacao, cream, sugar), and the Black Russian (vodka and coffee liqueur).

THE BLACK RUSSIAN AND THE WHITE are often said to be created by the same bartender, and the more I read the less I believe it: Both were likely created by liquor companies to sell coffee liqueurs.

Still, the story oft repeated is that the Black Russian (and sometimes the White) was created by a Brussels hotel bartender named Gustave Tops in honor of Perle Mesta, a Washington, DC, socialite who became the US ambassador to Luxembourg in 1949. But I haven't come across any proof, and though Mesta was the woman for whom the nickname "the hostess with the mostess" was coined, she was by most accounts an observant Christian Scientist who didn't drink.

There's a better clue in a 1972 profile of Señorita Maria del Pilar Guitierrez, Kahlúa's general manager in Mexico City. She mentions a Beverly Hills ad agency responsible for creating the recipe for the Black Russian around a dozen years earlier. This later date also jibes with what Dale DeGroff, perhaps the country's foremost cocktail expert, said about the drink in his 2008 book *The Essential Cocktail*:

"The Black Russian came into its own as a popular drink in the late 1960s and 1970s, the ebb tide of cocktails, when it was almost impossible to find fresh ingredients and well-made drinks," wrote DeGroff. "It was in these Dark Ages of mixology that vodka made its ascendance to the spirit of choice in America, and Kahlúa was the recipient of a heavy promotional budget that was wildly successful.... And so," he concluded, "back at this moment the extraordinarily simple Black Russian—a sweet drink that's not cloying, that could be taken before dinner as well as after—enjoyed its moment in the spotlight."

IF THE BLACK RUSSIAN WAS HALFWAY SOPHISTICATED— simple, sleek, all black—the White Russian never was. This melted ice cream cone of a cocktail first appeared, near as I can tell, in 1965 ads for a copycat Kahlua called Coffee Southern—along with recipes for the Black Russian, the Java Sundae, and the Southern Grasshopper. It appealed to "disco babies" of the late 1970s, explained DeGroff, "when a lot of people were awake at night with a craving for something sweet."

"When I first encountered it in the 1970s, the White Russian was something real alcoholics drank, or beginners," agreed cocktail historian David Wondrich in a 2008 *New York Times* article about the drink.

At that time, it had developed a newfound shine thanks to *The Big Lebowski*, the 1998 movie whose main character's* consumption of White Russians cemented this high-calorie cocktail into the foundation of modern American pop culture. It also made the drink "the mark of the hipster," as Mr. Wondrich observed.

Cocktail snobs still snub it, but it is now solidly in the American cultural canon, perhaps better known to most ordinary Americans than almost any other drink.

*The Dude, who did sometimes use half-and-half.

Below, Jeff Bridges as the Dude dreams of the original dude, a White Russian–drinking Seattle character named Jeff Dowd who inspired filmmakers Joel and Ethan Coen. At right, The White Russian first appeared in 1965, in magazine ads for a coffee-flavored liqueur produced by Southern Comfort; Kahlua was created in Mexico in 1936 and arrived in the United States a few years later.

THE DUDES

DR. ALLENE ROSALIND JEANES

XANTHAN GUM

Xanthan gum may not seem like the most reputable American food invention, given its usual role as one in a long list of head-scratching ingredients in processed foods. But this flavorless gelling agent and thickener has always been a game changer: It gives things a smoother, richer mouthfeel, keeps things from separating, and, in the case of Wish-Bone salad dressing, keeps all those herbs and spices suspended in the vinaigrette.

"Let us concentrate for a moment on the wonders of xanthan gum," wrote Thomas Vilgis in the 2012 cookbook *The Kitchen as Laboratory*, where he turns a tower of chopped veg into a savory flan with its help. "One reason xanthan is useful for so many industrial and culinary applications is that it is not much affected by acidity, salt content, or even temperature," he noted, adding that you don't need to use very much of it, either.

UNLESS YOU'RE GLUTEN-FREE or a molecular gastronomist (in which case you already know about the magical properties of this fermented substance to make wheat-free breads that don't bake up like bricks and to turn a liquid into a sauce or gel at any temperature), you might not think as highly of xanthan gum as Vilgis does.

"It's just this weird-sounding modern chemical name," said Wesley Stokes, who helps his wife, Robin, run Blazing Star Foods in western New Jersey. They considered including it in her gourmet salad dressings, he told me, but decided against it because they were afraid of what their customers might think.

Allene Rosalind Jeanes (1906–1995) was a groundbreaking American chemist and one of the few women at the top of her field in the mid-1900s. She was able to tame bacteria to create new substances that revolutionized several industries.

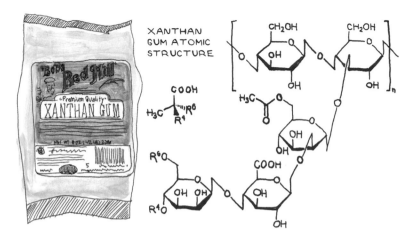

Early articles in the 1970s—when Xanthan gum was just coming onto the general marketplace—maybe didn't help. It was approved by the government in 1969, and in 1976, the *Tampa Bay Times* profiled a scientist at the Peoria, Illinois, research center for the US Department of Agriculture. The article, which included a not-very-attractive black-and-white photo of a squat loaf, focused on the scientist's wheat-free, soy-protein-packed xanthan gum bread made as a gluten-free meat substitute. (To quote the prescient scientist, whose name was Donald Christianson: "Everyone knows that meat is going to get uneconomical.")

XANTHAN GUM WAS DISCOVERED in the 1950s at the same lab, by a crack chemist originally from Waco, Texas. Her name was Allene Rosalind Jeanes, and she earned ten patents, a master's from Berkeley, a PhD from the University of Illinois, and, in 1953, the first Distinguished Service Award from the Department of Agriculture given to a woman.

Jeanes's specialty was isolating benefits from the bacteria that broke down a type of carbohydrate called polysaccharides, which include starches found in wheat, rice, potatoes, and corn. Her first polysaccharide discovery was used as a plasma substitute in the Korean and Vietnam wars. (Her eyes are closed in a 1962 photo with President Kennedy, when she posed with the other women who got a Federal Woman's Award for outstanding contributions to government. For some reason, that makes me like her even more.)

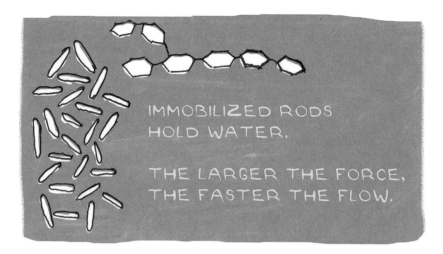

IMMOBILIZED RODS
HOLD WATER.

THE LARGER THE FORCE,
THE FASTER THE FLOW.

Later Jeanes led the team that figured out how unleash a specific kind of bacteria—*Xanthomonas campestris*, found in the rotten bits of tomatoes and broccoli—on glucose or fructose, which are sugars in their most basic form.

As the bacteria eat the sugars, their enzymes create a slimy coating. Add some rubbing alcohol, the slime separates from the bacteria, and—ta-da!—you've got xanthan gum. It's collected with a centrifuge, purified, and dried into a powder that anyone can now buy in a resealable pink bag from Bob's Red Mill. Or as a sleek tube of Texturas Xantana, the self-described "Rolls-Royce" of xanthan gums, marketed by Spanish chef and molecular gastronomy guy Ferran Adrià.

TO PUT IT ANOTHER WAY, xanthan gum is not that much creepier than your average fermentation project—as in vinegar, beer and wine, yogurt, or cheese—all of which rely on bacteria. It maybe just has an unglamorous name, though you have to admit it's light-years better than Sugar Slime, and maybe even better than Texturas Xantana.

TURMERIC

WHITE
MUSTARD
SEED

Yellow
Mustard

YELLOW MUSTARD

When R. T. French & Sons created yellow mustard in 1904, they were doing what Americans have so often done to foods from other places. They took a rustic, earthy, intensely flavored icon, then smoothed out the flavor and turned it Technicolor. But with yellow mustard—known in other parts of the world as American mustard—maybe that's a beautiful thing.

"This is an American comfort food," said Barry Levenson, an attorney, playwright, founder of the Mustard Museum in Middleton, Wisconsin, and one of yellow mustard's biggest fans. "When I go to a ball game the first thing I do is I get a hot dog, and I just hold it up to the sky," he said. "The blue sky, the green grass, the yellow mustard—that's what it's all about.

"We need to appreciate yellow mustard for what it is," he added. "It doesn't get the respect it deserves."

ANCIENT ROMANS WERE MAYBE THE FIRST to blend or roughly crush the piquant little mustard seeds with grape must to make condiments, and the French refined the idea once they created a machine to process seeds of the mustard plant into paste at great volumes. Listed in order of pungency, there are black mustard seeds, brown mustard seeds, and white mustard seeds, all of which are brassicas, like cabbage and broccoli.

Yellow mustard is rare in that it uses only the mild white seeds, which are combined with salt, plenty of vinegar, and turmeric, which gives it a little extra flavor but also makes it primary yellow. (French Dijon mustard is brown seeds plus wine; English Colman's, turmeric plus brown and white.)

R. T. FRENCH & SONS began life in the nineteenth century as a spice company, selling whole mustard seeds and powders. But then, according to a letter that may or may not be real, one French son (Francis) wrote to another (George) about his idea to make a new mustard: "One that is mild and has a true mustard flavor, and yet is light and creamy in consistency and color. There is no condiment like I have in mind on the market, and I'm sure that such a mustard, even if it costs ten dollars a gallon, would have a ready and wide sale. It must be mild, for I believe that these hot mustards are used sparingly not because they are hot, but because people do not like them."

THE COMPANY CALLED their new creation Cream Salad Mustard.* They packed it in glass jars inside a box with a wooden paddle and sold it like crazy. Sixty years later, yellow mustard was so popular in the States

---

*Supposedly if you just added cream, it made a delicious salad dressing.

that until Grey Poupon came along in the late 1970s (see Ketchup, page 77), yellow was often the only mustard in you could buy. And it's still the top-selling mustard in the country, if not the world.

YELLOW'S SUCCESS (and its plastic squeeze-y bottle) may be its achilles heel, says Levenson. Today it's not considered as gourmet as all the rough-hewn imports or chef-driven options labelled by hand, even though you recognize the name of every ingredient on its label. He thinks that's unfair.

Yellow mustard may not have the romance of a ceramic crock, he said, but it's tasty. It's smooth and piquant, tart and maybe a teeny bit bitter, a flavor that is actually ideal when blended into potato salad, stirred into salad dressing, or squirted on sharp cheese or a fatty frank. Not to mention its use of turmeric, whose anti-inflammatory properties have made it a super-popular modern ingredient.

"If it didn't exist, and some chef invented it now," said Levenson, "everyone would say 'Wow, brilliant.'"

MUSTARD OF A CERTAIN VINTAGE

Z
ZUCCHINI BREAD

"A few weeks ago, I received in the mail a recipe for Zucchini Bread," wrote Miriam Miller in the "Kitchen Komment" column of the Corvallis, Oregon, *Gazette-Times* of May 3, 1972. "It sounded pretty awful, I thought, so I threw it away. It wasn't until last week that I regretted my hasty act."

So goes the first public appearance of zucchini bread, as far as I can tell. Miller had been rubbing shoulders with an Oregon senator's wife—Mrs. Mark O. Hatfield, aka Antoinette Kuzmanich, who wrote a series of cookbooks called Remarkable Recipes from the Recipe File of Mrs. Mark O. Hatfield. When the two women met, Hatfield had just tasted zucchini bread at the home ec class at Tigard High School—some ten miles south of downtown Portland, Oregon—and she loved it. Luckily, she sent the recipe to Miller, and it ran in the paper two weeks later.

IT APPEARED IN SIMILAR FASHION in ladies' food columns in the northwest United States that year—in Alaska or northern California, with maybe a few nuts, some raisins, slightly different proportions, always secured from a local with sought-after skills (Marge Maita from Sacramento; Mary Hilliard in Sebastopol). It had snuck a little farther east by 1973, and then again by 1974, and by 1975 it was almost everywhere.

"The recipe for zucchini bread which has been going the rounds from bridge club to neighborhood kaffeeklatsch the past few years is delicious, a moist, sweet concoction that is more like a cake than a bread," wrote

---

Rainy Portland, Oregon, seems to be ground zero for zucchini bread, though zucchini itself is probably an Italian hybrid of a South American plant later cultivated by Italian-Americans in California.

Yvonne Rothert in 1975 in the *Oregonian*; she included four new ways to make it, including the semi-sweet granola-buttermilk version adapted on the opposite page.

BY THEN, THE RECIPE FOR "CARL GOHS' ZUCCHINI BREAD" had also been printed in James Beard's bestselling *Beard on Bread*, which was reprinted seven times in its first year alone. Beard got his recipe from Gohs, a friend from Portland, Oregon, where Beard grew up.

Gohs was also a food writer, a local-level Beard blessed by a friendship with the real one. He wrote for *Northwest*, the Sunday *Oregonian* magazine. He helped Beard teach his famed cooking classes at Seaside, helped editor Helen McCully on books about early American cooking, worked on Time Life series cookbooks on American cooking and the Northwest, and traveled with beard to France in 1972 to do work for *Beard on Bread*: "We stayed at Julia Child's house outside Cannes," he said in Beard's *Oregonian* obituary a decade later; "there he went over the manuscripts for the book. I scouted out French breads for his approval."

Gohs lived within walking distance of the paper, in a little apartment building with a green velvet staircase and vine-covered walls and a view of the city he loved below. From his columns, we know he was a renaissance man and an adventurous eater, that he led tours in Europe of food and architecture and was a good writer on many subjects, especially the Pacific Northwest, about which he created two beautiful books with the photographer Ray Atkeson. (One is called *Oregon*; the other, *Washington*.)

SO GOHS GOT AROUND. He could easily have read about zucchini bread in the Corvallis column, or been with Mrs. Mark O., or heard about it from the ladies' food scene. He could have been the one who gave the recipe to them, though that's doubtful. In fact, it seems like a funny twist that his most famous recipe got its start as a women's club classic, considering some of his best-known work was for an *Oregonian* Sunday magazine column called "Man in the Kitchen," where Gohs and others interviewed local dudes about what they cooked.

By 1972, as Beard worked away on his bread book, Gohs had manned up zucchini multiple times, though with no mention of anything like

ADAPTED FROM THE OREGONIAN

ZUCCHINI BREAD IV

½ CUP PACKED BROWN SUGAR	½ CUP VEGETABLE OIL
2 EGGS	1½ CUPS GRATED ZUCCHINI
½ CUP BUTTERMILK	1½ CUPS ALL-PURPOSE FLOUR
2 TSP BAKING POWDER	½ TEASPOON BAKING SODA
½ TEASPOON SALT	1½ CUPS GRANOLA

MIX SUGAR AND OIL IN LARGE MIXER BOWL. BEAT IN EGGS THOROUGHLY. MIX ZUCCHINI & BUTTERMILK. RESERVE. MIX FLOUR, BAKING POWDER, BAKING SODA, AND SALT. BEAT FLOUR MIXTURE INTO EGG MIXTURE, ALTERNATELY WITH ZUCCHINI MIXTURE, BEGINNING AND ENDING WITH FLOUR. FOLD IN GRANOLA. POUR INTO GREASED AND FLOURED 9X5" LOAF PAN. BAKE IN A 350-DEGREE OVEN FOR 55-60 MINUTES, OR UNTIL A TOOTHPICK INSERTED IN CENTER COMES OUT CLEAN. REMOVE FROM PAN IMMEDIATELY. COOL BEFORE SLICING.

MAN IN THE KITCHEN

CECI N'EST PAS UNE
ZUCCHINI

CARL
GOHS

CARL GOHS WAS MORE KNOWN FOR HIS PIPE SMOKING THAN HIS ZUCCHINI BREAD.

a quick bread. He penned eloquent little odes to zucchini's habit of overproducing in the garden—"the prolific tempter"—and how to turn the excess into a baked dish with chicken thighs, tomato sauce, and croutons. He wrote about "Hot Zucchini Salad," where you cook salami, zucchini, and torn romaine lettuce together in a cup of olive oil till it all wilts. There was also zucchini Colistro, a lasagna-like thing that uses a quarter pound of bacon, a pound of pork, a pound of ground beef, five medium to large zucchini, three cups of bread crumbs, plus mozzarella cheese. According to the recipe, it served four. (Which is about as Man in the Kitchen as it gets.)

HE WROTE ABOUT ZUCCHINI SO OFTEN that it is slightly odd he wasn't included in that 1975 story by Yvonne Rothert, who by that time may have even been one of his editors at the *Oregonian*. Strangely, for a story about so many ways to make zucchini bread, Rothert didn't mention the version that was credited to both local hero Beard and her colleague Gohs.

Then again, she didn't need to. It was identical to the ones that had already been shared by countless ladies of the Pacific Northwest over the past three years.

SELECTED BIBLIOGRAPHY

Albuquerque Tribune, eds. *New Mexico's Prized Recipes from The* Albuquerque Tribune's *Great Green Chili Cooking Classic.* The Albuquerque Tribune, 1974.

Anderson, Jean. *A Love Affair with Southern Cooking.* William Morrow, 2007.

Arthur, Stanley Clisby, *Famous New Orleans Drinks and How to Mix 'Em.* Pelican Press, 1937.

Barringer, Maria. *Dixie Cookery: Or How I Managed My Table for Twelve Years, for Southern Housekeepers.* Loring, 1867.

Beard, James. *Beard on Bread.* Alfred A. Knopf, 1995. (Originally published 1973.)

———. *The James Beard Cookbook.* Dell Publishing Co., 1959.

Belasco, Warren. *Meals to Come: A History of the Future of Food.* University of California Press, 2006.

Better Homes and Gardens, eds. *Better Homes and Gardens Meat Cook Book.* Meredith Corporation, 1969.

———. *Better Homes and Gardens Mexican Cook Book.* Meredith Corporation, 1977.

Boni, Ada. *The Talisman Italian Cook Book.* Crown Publishers, 1960.

Bovino, Arthur. *Buffalo Everything: A Guide to Eating in "The Nickel City."* Countryman Press, 2018.

Brown, Dale. *Foods of the World: American Cooking.* Time-Life Books, 1968.

Brown, Edward Espe. *The Tassajara Bread Book.* Shambhala Publications, 1970.

Byrn, Anne. *American Cake: From Colonial Gingerbread to Classic Layer, the Story Behind Our Best-Loved Cakes from Past to Present.* Rodale Books, 2016.

Cannon, Poppy. *The New Can-Opener Cookbook.* Thomas Y. Crowell Company, 1959. (Originally published 1951.)

Child, Lydia Marie. *The Frugal Housewife.* Andrews McMeel, 2013. (Originally published 1829.)

Claiborne, Craig. *Craig Claiborne's Favorites from The New York Times: Recipes, restaurants, tools, techniques, people, and places.* Times Books, 1975.

Clark, Mrs. Arthur, Jr. *Bayou Cuisine: Its Tradition and Transition.* St. Stephen's Episcopal Church, 1972. (Originally published 1970.)

Clifton, Denise E. *Tables from the Rubble: How the Restaurants That Arose After the Great Quake Still Feed San Francisco Today.* Tandemvines, 2017.

Collin, Rima, and Richard Collin. *The New Orleans Cookbook.* Alfred A. Knopf, 2004. (Originally published 1975.)

Counihan, Carole M. *Food in the USA: A Reader.* Routledge, 2002.

Crosby, Alfred W. *The Columbian Exchange: Biological and Cultural Consequences of 1492.* Praeger, 2006. (Originally published 1972.)

Davidow, Claire S., and Ann Goodman. *Pennsylvania Dutch Cookbook of Fine Old Recipes.* Culinary Arts Books, 1987. (Originally published 1960.)

Davidson, Alan. *The Oxford Companion to Food,* 2nd ed. Oxford University Press, 2006.

DeGroff, Dale. *The Essential Cocktail.* Clarkson Potter, 2008.

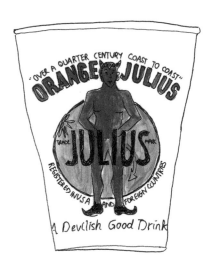

A Devilish Good Drink

Hess, Karen. *The Carolina Rice Kitchen: The African Connection.* University of South Carolina Press, 2008. (Originally published 1992.)

Hughes, Phyllis. *Pueblo Indian Cookbook.* Museum of New Mexico Press, 1977. (Originally published 1972.)

Iammarino, Alexis, and Maeve O'Regan. *Hole History, Origins of the American-Style Donut.* Little Legs Production, 2018.

Jaramillo, Cleofas M. *The Genuine New Mexico Tasty Recipes.* Ancient City Press, 1981. (Originally published 1939.)

Jones, Evan. *American Food: The Gastronomic Story.* The Overlook Press, 2007. (Originally published 2007.)

Junior League of Lafayette Louisiana, eds. *Talk About Good.* The Wimmer Companies, 1995. (Originally published 1967.)

Kennedy, Diana. *My Mexico: A Culinary Odyssey with Recipes.* University of Texas Press, 2013. (Originally published 1998.)

Khong, Rachel, and the editors of Lucky Peach. *All About Eggs.* Clarkson Potter, 2017.

La Cocinera Poblana y el Libro de las Familias. J. F. Jens, 1887. (In Spanish; originally published 1872.)

LaFrieda, Pat, and Carolyn Carreño. *Meat: Everything You Need to Know.* Atria Books, 2014.

Dougherty, Richard. *In Quest of Quality: Hormel's First 75 Years.* Geo. A. Hormel & Co., 1966.

Edge, John T. *Donuts: An American Passion.* G.P. Putnam Sons, 2005.

Fain, Lisa. *QUESO! Regional Recipes for the World's Favorite Chile-Cheese Dip.* Ten Speed Press, 2017.

Fox, Minnie C. *The Blue Grass Cook Book,* with Bluegrass and Black Magic: An Introduction to the New Edition by Toni Tipton-Martin. University Press of Kentucky, 2015. (Originally published 1904.)

Florence, Tyler. *Inside the Test Kitchen: 120 New Recipes, Perfected.* Clarkson Potter, 2014.

Gilbert, Fabiola Cabeza de Baca. *The Good Life: New Mexico Traditions and Food.* Museum of New Mexico Press, 2005. (Originally published 1981.)

Gourmet, Inc., eds. *The Gourmet Cookbook Volume II.* Gourmet Distributing Corporation, 1959. (Originally published 1957.)

Grimes, William. *Appetite City: A Culinary History of New York.* North Point Press, 2009.

Freedman, Paul, Joyce E. Chaplin, and Ken Albala Harris. *Food in Time and Place: The American Historical Association Companion to Food History.* University of California Press, 2014.

Haley, James L. *Captive Paradise: A History of Hawaii.* St. Martin's Griffin, 2015.

Langholtz, Gabrielle. *America the Cookbook.* Phaidon Press, 2017.

Lee, Jennifer 8. *The Fortune Cookie Chronicles. Adventures in the World of Chinese Food.* Twelve, 2008.

Leslie, Eliza. *Seventy-Five Receipts for Pastry, Cakes & Sweetmeats.* Andrews McMccl, 2013. (Originally published 1835.)

Levine, Ed. *Pizza: A Slice of Heaven.* Universe, 2005.

Levenstein, Harvey. *Revolution at the Table: The Transformation of the American Diet.* University of California Press, 2003.

Lustig, Lillie, S. Claire Sondheim, and Sarah Rensel. *The Southern Cook Book of Fine Old Recipes.* Culinary Arts Press, 1939.

Mackie, Christine. *Life and Food in the Caribbean.* New Amsterdam, 1991.

Macmillan, Diane D. *The Portable Feast.* 101 Productions, 1973.

Maui Extension Homemakers' Council, eds. *Our Golden Anniversary Favorite Recipes.* Maui Extension Homemakers' Council, 1980.

McWilliams, James E. *A Revolution in Eating: How the Quest for Food Shaped America.* Columbia University Press, 2005.

Medrano, Adán. *Truly Texas Mexican: A Native Culinary Heritage in Recipes.* Texas Tech University Press, 2014.

Mendelson, Anne. *Stand Facing the Stove: The Story of the Women Who Gave America the Joy of Cooking.* Scribner, 2003. (Originally published 1996.)

Meyer, Adolphe. *Eggs and How to Use Them.* Self-published, 1898.

Miller, Adrian. *Soul Food: The Surprising Story of an American Cuisine, One Plate at a Time.* The University of North Carolina Press, 2013.

Nichols, Nell B. *Homemade Bread: By the Food Editors of Farm Journal.* Doubleday and Company, 1969.

Parks, Stella. *Bravetart: Iconic American Desserts.* W. W. Norton & Company, 2017.

Peterson, James. *Fish & Shellfish.* William Morrow, 1996.

Picayune, The (New Orleans), eds. *The Picayune's Creole Cook Book.* Andrews McMeel, 2013. (Originally published 1901.)

Randolph, Mary. *The Virginia Housewife.* Andrews McMeel, 2013. (Originally published 1828.)

Ranhoter, Charles. *The Epicurean.* Self-published, 1894.

Ranhofer, Charles, and Rose Ranhofer. *The Epicurean.* Self-published, 1912.

———. *The Epicurean.* The Hotel Monthly Press, 1920.

Richardson, Julie. *Vintage Cakes.* Ten Speed Press, 2012.

Robinson, Sallie Ann. *Cooking the Gullah Way, Morning, Noon, and Night.* The University of North Carolina Press, 2007.

Robinson, Sallie Ann. *Gullah Home Cooking the Daufuskie Way: Smokin' Joe Butter Beans, Ol' 'Fuskie Fried Crab Rice, Sticky-Bush Blackberry Dumpling, and Other Sea Island Favorites.* The University of North Carolina Press, 2003.

Rombauer, Irma S., and Marion Rombauer Becker. *Joy of Cooking*. Bobbs-Merrill Company, 1984. (Originally published 1975.)

Sammarco, Anthony Mitchell. *A History of Howard Johnson's: How a Massachusetts Soda Fountain Became an American Icon*. American Palate, 2013.

Santlofer, Joy. *Food City: Four Centuries of Food-Making in New York*. W. W. Norton & Company, 2016.

Shapiro, Laura. *Perfection Salad: Women and Cooking at the Turn of the Century*. California Studies in Food and Culture, 2008.

Shepherd, Gordon M. *Neurogastronomy: How the Brain Creates Flavor and Why It Matters*. Columbia University Press, 2012.

Shilling, Donovan A. *Made in Rochester*. Pancoast, 2015.

Schuler, Stanley, and Elizabeth Meriwether Schuler. *Preserving the Fruits of the Earth: How to "Put Up" Almost Every Food Grown in the United States in Almost Every Way*. Galahad Books, 1973.

Smalls, Alexander, JJ Johnson, and Veronica Chambers. *Between Harlem and Heaven*. Flatiron Books, 2018.

Smith, Andrew F. *The Encyclopedia of Food and Drink in America*, vols. 1 and 2. Oxford University Press, 2004.

Smith, Jeff. *The Frugal Gourmet on Our Immigrant Ancestors: Recipes You Should Have Gotten from Your Grandmothers*. William Morrow, 1990.

Sohn, Mark F. *Appalachian Home Cooking: History, Culture, and Recipes*. University Press of Kentucky, 2005.

Steen, Mrs. J. Wesley. *The Story of Steen's Syrup and Its Famous Recipes*. C. S. Steen Syrup Company, 1981.

Steinberg, Sally Levitt. *The Donut Book*. Storey Publishing, 2004.

Swentzell, Roxanne, and Patricia M. Perea. *The Pueblo Food Experience Cookbook*. Museum of New Mexico Press, 2016.

Tipton-Martin, Toni. *The Jemima Code: Two Centuries of African American Cookbooks*. University of Texas Press, 2015.

Toklas, Alice B. *The Alice B. Toklas Cook Book*. Anchor Books, 1960. (Originally published 1954.)

Tschirky, Oscar. *The Cook Book by Oscar of the Waldorf*. The Smithfield Publishing Co., 1896.

Twitty, Michael W. *The Cooking Gene: A Journey Through African American Culinary History in the Old South*. HarperCollins, 2017.

U.S. Department of Agriculture. *How to Buy Beef Steaks: Consumer and Marketing Service Home and Garden Bulletin No. 145*. U.S. Department of Agriculture, 1968.

van Willigen, John, and Anne van Willigen. *Food and Everyday Life on Kentucky Family Farms, 1920–1950*. University Press of Kentucky, 2006.

Vega, César, Job Ubbink, and Erik van der Linden. *The Kitchen as Laboratory: Reflections on the Science of Food and Cooking*. Columbia University Press, 2012.

Veit, Helen Zoe. *Food in the Civil War Era: The South*. Michigan State University Press, 2015.

Walker, Barbara M. *The Little House Cookbook: Frontier Foods from Laura Ingalls Wilder's Classic Stories*. Harper & Row, 1979.

Willis, Virginia. *Bon Appétit, Y'all*. Ten Speed Press, 2008.

Wyoming Recreation Commission, eds. *Cooking in Wyoming*. Bighorn Book Company, 1965.

Yang, Winnie. *Fat Is Flavor v 2.0.: The Most Important Meal of the Day Is All of Them*. Self-published, 2008.

ACKNOWLEDGMENTS

First and foremost, we both thank (and would never have done this without) our mutual friend Rachel Corbett, who listened to Kim's wishes to work on a food book that didn't have photographs and thought to introduce us.

We thank our agent, David Patterson, and his Stuart Krichevsky Literary Agency colleagues like Aemilia Phillips and Hannah Schwartz for helping us bring this not-so-serious project to life, as well as our entire excellent team at Abrams: editor numero uno Holly Dolce, managing editor Lisa Silverman, designer Eli Mock, creative chiefs John Gall and Deb Wood, and production manager Anet Sirna-Bruder.

KIM ALSO THANKS: The near-mythical quote from Maira Kalman about how a painting is truer than a photograph, which has always been my guiding light. And the students I teach in the MFA in Illustration Practice program at MICA are always reminding me why we draw.

So many of the foods we considered for each letter were inspired by the input of friends and neighbors. Brooke Petry sent me hundreds of selections, and I still wish we could do them all! Thanks to Ms. Pat, the retired crossing guard from our neighborhood, for the hoagie direction, and to Lou Sarcone Jr. for his generosity with his bakery. Terri, Heather, Jeanine, Donna, Christine, Ryan, Jim, Sue, and most especially Lauren and Billy sent me stories of their memories of Orange Julius. Thank you! And quick thanks to the wallpaper installer in Wilmington, Delaware, who introduced me to the Bobbie sandwich.

Thanks to my mom, who taught me to cook and left me free to roam her kitchen. This inspired my love of small-town cookbooks and eventually led me to this book. I am especially grateful to all the writers of weird homemade recipes out there. You are my favorites. And to my husband and daughters, thanks for eating all the weird things I cook.

Thanks for reference photographs are also due to Lou's Sandwich Shop, the creator of the zep Italian sandwich, in Norristown, Pennsylvania, for the image of their counter on page 60; the former hoop cheese highway sign from Ada's "The Universal" Country Store in Bethel

Springs, Tennessee, for the images on page 89; the Rock Hall Library and Archive for the Beastie Boys portrait on page 107; the Institute of Texan Cultures for the *casera* ladies image on page 118, the Isle of Wight County Museum for the World's Oldest Ham on page 124, and Portland Oregon's Arlene Schnitzer Concert Hall and the Town Club for the opening collage of the Zucchini chapter. Thanks also to the lunch counter at Duran Central Pharmacy in New Mexico, which posed for our cover illustration.

RACHEL ALSO THANKS: Those who make and grow and write about food in this country, especially those whose contributions are and were overlooked in our short history. I especially thank those who gave me their time and knowledge, I am constantly amazed people are generous enough to answer my many questions. I tried to give you all credit by name where it really counts, in the stories you helped illuminate.

I thank my parents, Linda and Lane, for instilling in me the curiosity and open mind every good journalist needs, and my dad especially for taking me on all those side trips and excursions that are essentially what I now do for a living. And my sister, Rebekah, for being amazing, and John Taggart for always coming with me. (I'll come with you when you do your own book, too.)

AND A VERY LAST SHOUT-OUT from Kim to Rachel and from Rachel to Kim for your collaboration, openness, and enthusiasm for everything in this book!!!

INDEX

Editor: Holly Dolce
Designer: Eli Mock
Production Manager: Anet Sirna-Bruder

Library of Congress Control Number: 2018958837

ISBN: 978-1-4197-3814-2
eISBN: 978-1-68335-678-3

Printed and bound in the United States

10 9 8 7 6 5 4 3 2 1

Abrams Image books are available at special discounts when
purchased in quantity for premiums and promotions as well as
fundraising or educational use. Special editions can also be created
to specification. For details, contact specialsales@abramsbooks.com
or the address below.

Abrams Image® is a registered trademark of Harry N. Abrams, Inc.

ABRAMS The Art of Books
195 Broadway, New York, NY 10007
abramsbooks.com